THE CHINESE OF SARAWAK

LONDON SCHOOL OF ECONOMICS MONOGRAPHS ON SOCIAL ANTHROPOLOGY

Managing Editor: Charles Stafford

The Monographs on Social Anthropology were established in 1940 and aim to publish results of modern anthropological research of primary interest to specialists.

The continuation of the series was made possible by a grant in aid from the Wenner-Gren Foundation for Anthropological Research, and more recently by a further grant from the Governors of the London School of Economics and Political Science. Income from sales is returned to a revolving fund to assist further publications.

The Monographs are under the direction of an Editorial Board associated with the Department of Anthropology of the London School of Economics and Political Science.

THE CHINESE OF SARAWAK

A STUDY OF SOCIAL STRUCTURE

JU-K'ANG T'IEN

LONDON SCHOOL OF ECONOMICS MONOGRAPHS ON SOCIAL ANTHROPOLOGY

Volume 12

Oxford • New York

Published in 2004 by

Berg

Editorial Offices:
1st Floor, Angel Court, 81 St Clements Street, Oxford OX4 1AW, UK
175 Fifth Avenue, New York, NY 10010, USA

Previously published by

The London School of Economics and Political Science
London, UK

Berg is an imprint of Oxford International Publishers Ltd.

ISBN 1 84520 011 X (Cloth)

Printed in the United Kingdom by Biddles Ltd, King's Lynn

www.bergpublishers.com

T A B L E   O F   C O N T E N T S

		Page
I	The Problem	1
II	Emigration and Emigrants ...	2
III	The Warp and Woof of Chinese Associations ...	10
IV	The Nature of the Chinese Community ...	19
V	Clanship	21
VI	Rural Economy and Clan Relationships ...	35
VII	Occupational Identification and Bazaar Economy	45
VIII	Bazaar Economy and the Rubber Trade ...	58
IX	The Problem of Power	68
X	Relations with the Mother Country ...	79
APPENDIX I	The Early History of the Chinese in Sarawak	(omitted)
APPENDIX II	The Hakka Kongsi in Borneo	(omitted)
APPENDIX III	Chinese population by dialect groups (Table)	90 – 91

L I S T   O F   M A P S

			Facing Page
1.	SARAWAK:	ADMINISTRATIVE DIVISIONS	2
2.	SOUTHERN CHINA:	THE PROVINCES OF KWANGTUNG AND FUKIEN. Showing approximate place of origin of different dialect groups.	12
3.	SARAWAK:	KUCHING-BAU-SERIAN AREA OF 1st DIVISION: Distribution of Chinese according to locality of origin.	32

LIST   OF   TABLES   AND   DIAGRAMS

Page	Table	
3	1	Land and Population in Kwangtung.
16	2	Dominant Groups in Three Small Chinese Associations in Kuching.
16	3	Dominant Groups among the Chinese Associations in Kuching.
18	3A	Dominant Clans of Dominant Groups of Chinese Associations in Kuching.
27	4	T'ien Clan in Sarawak 1949.
28	5	Names and Number of Members of Hoppu Clans.
30	6	Clan Relationships of Oversea Chinese living along the Simanggang Road.
32	7	Clan Relationships Among the Oversea Chinese Living along the Road from Kuching to Bau.
33	7A	Clan Relationships Among the Oversea Chinese Living in the Coastal Areas of the First Division.
Facing 34	8	Distribution of Ts'ai clan members along the Simanggang Road (1949).
36	9	Distance From School.
46	10	Ownership of Chinese Shops in Kuching.
48-49	11	Relationship Between Dialect Similarity and Occupational Grouping in Kuching.
51	12	Occupational Identification in Sibu.
53	13	The Coffee Shop Business.
55	14	Ladder of Rubber Transactions Among the Overseas Chinese in Sarawak.
56	15	Dialect Differences Among the Rubber Dealers of Different Ranks.
57	16	Dialect and Occupation.
57	17	Dialect and Economic Status.
60	18	Export Duty Paid On Local Products July/November 1948.
61	19	Relations between Exporters in Kuching and Dealers in Singapore.
62	20	Cost per picul of Rubber Exported.
67	21	Import Relationships between First Division Sarawak and Singapore.
81	22	Chinese Publications dealing with Home News available in Sarawak.
83	23	Family Remittances to China through Approved Collecting Agents.
90-91	APPENDIX III	The Chinese Population of Sarawak: Dialect Groups (From the Census Report 1947).

A U T H O R ' S   P R E F A C E

The problems of the Chinese overseas -- particularly in South East Asia-- are of pressing significance at the present time. The most satisfactory study would embrace a full account of the relations of the overseas Chinese with foreign governments and with indigenous peoples.This would require a far-flung and detailed comparative survey for which I have neither the time nor the competence. Instead, I have taken one small field -- the oversea Chinese community in Sarawak -- and concentrated upon certain aspects only of its social life. If I am accused of omission, of looking at the trees and failing to see the forest, then I must plead guilty, but it is my hope that here in microcosm may be seen more clearly some of the factors which operate throughout the area.

Under the auspices of the Colonial Social Science Research Council I spent about thirteen months in Sarawak from September 1948 to October 1949. My mandate was to study the role of 'associations' in the Chinese Community. I am deeply grateful for the numberless friends informants and officials who gave me their confidence, their time and their help.In London I have received every possible assistance, especially from Dr. E. R. Leach whose constructive criticism fell on almost every page of my manuscript, from Professor R.W. Firth, whose interest has been my encouragement, from Dr. D. Schneider and Mrs. N. Richardson. who read and commented upon several chapters, from Mr. R. van der Sprenkel, who tirelessly translated from the Dutch,and from Mrs. E.M. Chilver, who smoothed my official path. Last but certainly not least I must express my debt to Miss Barbara E.Ward who was my close collaborator throughout the period of final drafting. It is not easy for a Chinese to make himself fully comprehensible in the idiom of English scholarship. If I have achieved that end the credit is due to Miss Ward rather than myself.

JU-K'ANG T'IEN

London, June 1950.

E D I T O R I A L   P R E F A C E

The account of the Chinese of Sarawak given in this book is a slightly amended version of a report submitted to the Sarawak Government in the Summer of 1950 under the title 'A Report on the Organisation of the Chinese Community in Sarawak'.

The research of which this Report was the product was sponsored by the Colonial Social Science Research Council. While the Council has given permission for Dr T'ien's material to appear in its present form it needs to be stressed that the Council members are in no way responsible,either collectively or individually, for the views here expressed. Nor should it be supposed that Dr T'ien's views coincide in any way with those of the Sarawak Government or of any of its members.

E.R.L.

London. May 1953.

THE PROBLEM

Altogether there are about ten million Chinese overseas.[1] Nearly one third of them live in territories in South East Asia for which the British people are at present responsible. Westerners who think about them at all are likely to hold strong views. The Chinese are at one and the same time the backbone of Malaya and the Jews of the Orient; without them nothing could have been done, with them there is always potential danger. "Modern Malaya is built on coolie bones" or "the colony is a milch cow fed by the European, while the Chinese take all the milk": which is right? Opinions are easily made. At the present time the whole of South East Asia is undergoing one of the most rapid processes of social change that the world has ever seen: the indigenous peoples growing in political self-consciousness, the Chinese insecure, the European powers at a loss. All are apprehensive of the future. It is easy to hunt for scape-goats, and to find what you are looking for is never difficult. Most of the current discussion proceeds from opinion to opinion, but the hard fact is that very little is really known about the actual social situation in the Chinese communities overseas.

Moreover the Chinese communities themselves are changing, and rapidly, their changes necessarily affecting other groups of people, indigenous and European. Indeed it would not be entirely misleading to suggest that many of the sources of social change in South East Asia as a whole lie in changes in the communities of overseas Chinese. They are, in fact, geared into the whole complex of Asia wide social change, and they are not simple. The complexity of the facts makes all facile generalisations in purely political terms unrealistic. The Chinese are neither all "political agitators" nor all "apathetic". They are members of particular social groups in particular social situations, and their actions are explicable only in terms of that membership and those situations. Sociologists would be the first to agree that there are urgent problems here; but the current political manifestations are symptoms of something much deeper. The problems are social and economic, and require economic and sociological analysis.

The present work is intended as a contribution to the study of Chinese communities. Here in South East Asia are immigrant Chinese faced with geographical, economic and social challenges which are essentially different from those of China. Equipped with their Chinese social experience, these immigrant communities respond to the challenge of the new environment, and to its constant changes, in certain ways. The problem I have set myself is to discover what is the form of this response. The field chosen for this study is the First Division of the British Colony of Sarawak. This is a small area, recently opened up, its economic development still in the earliest stages. The 1947 Census[2] counted 145,158 Chinese in Sarawak as a whole, of whom 62,121 were in the First Division. These are small numbers in comparison with the 1,884,534 Chinese of Malaya[3] or the 730,133 of Singapore.[3] I cannot claim, therefore, that I am studying the problems of the overseas Chinese as a whole, still less the problems of such a world commercial centre as Singapore. I am simply studying a Chinese community in a Colonial territory in the first stages of capital accumulation. Although it is hoped that my findings may be of some help to those who are interested in the problems of the Chinese in other fields, it must be clearly recognized that none of the conclusions I may reach here will necessarily be applicable to communities in different territories and under different economic conditions.[4]

---

1. V. Purcell reckons nearly nine million in South East Asia alone.
2. Census Report, Sarawak. Kuching 1947.
3. Census Report, Malaya and Singapore. Singapore 1947.
4. When my research was carried out rubber was selling in Singapore at the equivalent of about 11 d. per lb.; at the time when I finished writing my report (May 1950) the price was about 1s.10d. per lb.; during the next twelve months it went very much higher but by August 1952 it had relapsed again to around 1s. per lb.

The First Division of Sarawak contains both rural and urban areas. These two types of social environment are economically interdependent. The rural districts depend upon the urban, or bazaar, centres for the distribution of imported goods; the bazaar centres depend upon the rural districts for the collection of primary produce for export. Closely interconnected though they are, the two types of area are sociologically strikingly different from each other. Speaking generally, they are inhabited by different dialect groups, and carry on their social activities through different types of social organisation. It is essential, therefore, to analyse their differences separately while recognizing their interdependence. The selection of Kuching for the urban area to be studied was made because Kuching, more than any other bazaar centre, contains samples of nearly all the different dialect groups, and thus presents the most comprehensive picture for the study of relations between these groups. It is important to note that in this respect Kuching differs entirely from most of the other urban centres in Sarawak where a single dialect group usually predominates. In Sibu, for instance, two-thirds of the population is Foochow speaking. Sibu, of course, is in the Third Division, but although I have concentrated my study upon the First Division I have not confined my interests to it alone, and where it seems helpful, or where there appear to be striking differences, I have drawn upon illustrative material from other Divisions.

The data from which this study has been compiled were collected partly from interviews, conversations and observations made in Sarawak between August 1948 and October 1949, and partly from documentary sources. The latter include published works in Chinese and European languages, and the unpublished records in government files, and in many associations and schools in Sarawak which were kindly made available to me. As a personal investigator I, being a Chinese, had both advantages and disadvantages. On the one hand my racial characteristics made me socially inconspicuous. My mother tongue is the variety of Mandarin spoken in Kunming (Yunnan Province, S.W. China). This differs only in minor ways from the National Language now taught in all Chinese schools both in China and in South East Asia. Thus I had no difficulty anywhere in Sarawak in conversing with educated Chinese. I could also manage to converse directly with uneducated individuals of the Southern Mandarin and Hakka dialect groups. I conversed with the uneducated of other dialect groups through a Mandarin speaking member of the group in question. Thus my native speech and my familiarity with the background of Chinese culture allowed me to concentrate from the very start upon the sociological problems I had in mind. On the other hand, as a Chinese I have certain natural sympathies and prejudices. Clearly this gives me a bias. An added difficulty was that my research was officially sponsored. This often made my personal position embarrassing. The objectives of my enquiry thus became matters for suspicion among Chinese and Europeans alike.

But let the reader be assured that I have tried to write this book only as a scientist. My task is analysis not criticism. I have tried to present the facts in such a way that they will speak for themselves. Any merits that this book possesses derive alike from the cooperation of Chinese informants and European officials, and I am grateful for that help and cooperation.

II

E M I G R A T I O N   A N D   E M I G R A N T S

It is well-known that nearly all the Chinese in the Nan Yang[1] came from the provinces of Fukien and Kwangtung. In Fukien there is a saying: Out of every ten who go abroad, three die, six remain, and only one comes home. Yet it is the ambition of every emigrant to return to the land of his forefathers. Why do they go at all? The obvious answer is that they go to seek their

1. "South Seas" the Common Chinese expression for all the territories of South East Asia to which Chinese have emigrated.

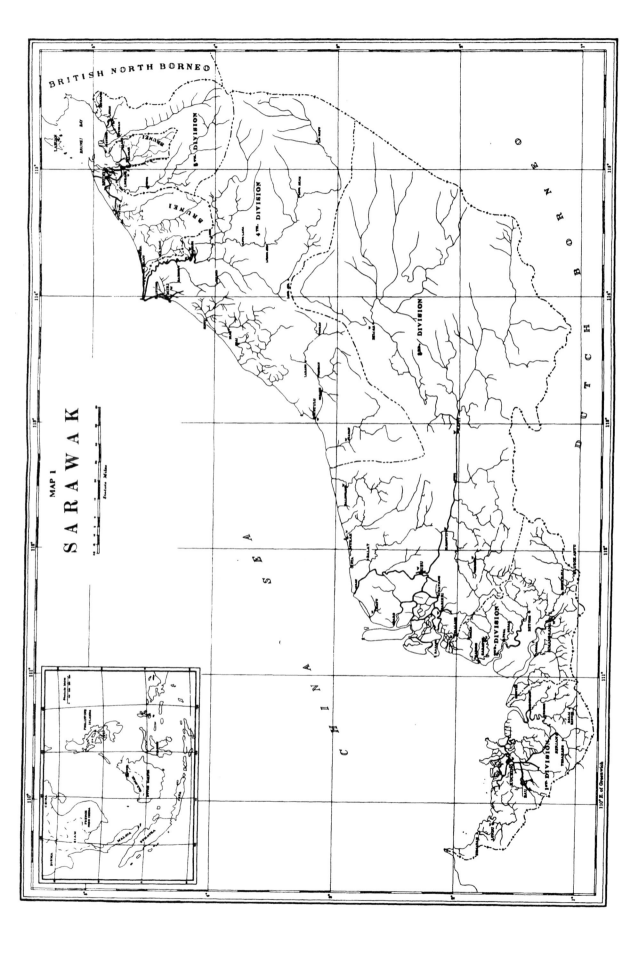

MAP 1
SARAWAK

fortunes. The movement is not designed to build up new lands, to create permanent communities overseas, like the British Dominions in New Zealand and Australia; it is an unplanned by-product of the overgrowth of population in China and the opportunity for travel offered by proximity to the sea and trading vessels.

China's swollen population has been the constant theme of Chinese and Western social studies. The pressure of population upon land appears to be greatest in Hunan, Kiangsi, Chekiang, Fukien and Kwangtung.[1] Over-population in Fukien was remarked at least in Sung times (960 - 1278 A.D.)[2], and certain districts of Fukien and Kwangtung have a particularly heavy pressure of population to this day. This is no doubt partly due to the large proportion of uncultivable land in these two provinces: in Fukien only 11%[3] and in Kwangtung only 7%[4] of the total area is worth cultivating. In Kwangtung the 12 hsiens[5] with the smallest proportion of cultivable land are:-

T A B L E   I

LAND AND POPULATION IN KWANGTUNG

Name of hsien	Amt. of cult. land(in shih mow) [6]	Percentage of total area [6]	Population 7	Density per mow of cult. land
1 Hsingning*	86,200	2.40	467,698	5.43
2 Tap'u (Tappu)	111,400	3.30	262,104	2.37
3 Wuhua *	139,800	3.65	327,786	2.35
4 P'ingyuan *	145,600	5.45		
5 Hsuwen	197,800	6.10		
6 Mei *	380,200	7.25	511,360	1.34
7 Chiaoling *	111,100	8.35	104,361	0.94
8 Haik'ang [8]	344,800	9.00		
9 Enp'ing	299,900	9.20		
10 Hweilai	302,600	10.55	255,719	0.84
11 Lufong	522,200	11.15		
12 Chaop'ing	434,111	13.55		

Certain areas of Fukien province, especially near Foochow, are comparatively rich,but elsewhere, for instance in the south,near Changchow "the soil

1. Including Hainan island. The China Year Book 1936-1937, Table I,(p.1253) Shanghai, 1937.
2. Sung Shih: Economic Section.
3. Chang hai-Yu: "The Industrialisation of Fukien" (in Chinese). Social Sciences, vol: 2 Nos. 1 - 2. (Institute of Social Sciences Fukien Academy.) 1946. p.115.
4. The Chinese Economic Year Book (in Chinese). (Shanghai) 1934 Section G p.235.
5. The "hsien" is an administrative area corresponding roughly to the English "county".
6. The Chinese Economic Year Book, (op. cit.) Section F. pp.51-52.
7. Report of Kwangtung Flood Relief Committee, (Canton) 1948. p.12.
8. Haik'ang hsien is on Hainan island. The total population of Hainan has been estimated at 2,500,000. Annual rice production, however, is sufficient only for 1,500,000. Ch'eng Chih: "The Solution of the Food Problem in Hainan" (in Chinese). Eastern Miscellany, vol:44, No.7, 1948, pp.22-25.
*   These 5 hsiens make up the Kiaying department of Kwangtung Province. As we shall see later a particularly large number of overseas Chinese in Sarawak come from Kiaying, Tap'u and Hweilai.

is very poor and of the cultivated land only 40% - 50% is suitable for rice. Most of it is sandy, suitable only for root crops. For this reason, even when the weather is favourable, the rice harvest yields only enough for half a year's consumption.

The major problem of the people here is not the price of rice, but its non-existence".[1]

Kwangtung and Fukien have long been importers of foodstuffs. Kwangtung draws rice from Kwangsi; Fukien from Kiangsi, Chiangsi and Formosa. Even so, a large proportion of peasant diet is made up of sweet potatoes. The fact that the sweet potato was apparently known in Fukien in the Ming dynasty is witness both to the urgent need of the Fukienese to find new crops and to their ability to profit from contact with the world outside China.[2]

Poverty and overpopulation explain only the impulse to emigrate; they do not explain the connection with the Nan Yang. There have been similar migrations from other parts of China. From the North Chinese have moved into Manchuria; from the South West into Burma; from Kwangtung and Fukien into the Nan Yang and the Americas. It is not necessary to look for reasons other than geographical proximity and historical opportunity.

Knowledge of the countries of the South Seas existed in the ports of Kwangtung and Fukien from a very early period. Chinese trade with the Indian Archipelago antedates European contacts by many centuries. The trading voyages were made coastwise by junks based upon Southern ports. Already in the T'ang and Sung dynasties there were official superintendents of merchant shipping in appointments at Canton, Chienchow (Fukien), Hanchow (Chekiang) and Yangchow (Kiansu). The Chu Fan Chi, written in the thirteenth century, describes this Southern trade in some detail.[3] European traders when they came. were practically confined to the ports of Kwantung and Fukien,[4] and information about opportunities overseas naturally came in there.

Thus when emigration to the Nan Yang began it was the people of Kwangtung and Fukien who had both the greatest incentives and the greatest opportunities. As we shall see later it is a characteristic of this Chinese migration that people from a particular district in China tend to congregate together in a particular district overseas. Once a stream of emigration has begun, it tends to continue to flow from the same source; the fact that it was people from Kwangtung and Fukien who had the initial opportunities to seek their fortunes

1. The Topography of Fukien (in Chinese). Vol:52.1821-1851. Many informants in Sarawak agreed that whatever their present difficulties they were at least able to eat full rice meals at last.
2. The sweet potato (Chinese: Fan ch'u. Ipomoea Batatas)originates from South America. It is commonly supposed to have reached China with the Portuguese, or through trading contacts after the European discovery of the New World. This Ming reference is to be found in: Ming Hsiao Chi (A short record of Fukien) written by one Chou Liang Kung and reprinted in the Ts'ung Shu Chi Cheng, (Shanghai,) 1936. Even in Sung times it was known that the people of Fukien had special crops. The Sung Shu tells of an imperial command to the governor of Chekiang at a time of drought in the year 1008, telling him to send to Fukien for seeds of a special variety of early rice which the Fukienese had earlier obtained from Indo-China. A Ch'ing Emperor (Yung Cheng 1723 - 1736), noting the small quantity of rice produced in Kwangtung and Fukien, and the relatively high development of such crops as sugar cane and tobacco, denounced the people of these two provinces as "avaricious" - a remark worthy of Marie Antoinette. Topography of Fukien, op. cit., Vol. I. See also (in English) L. Carrington-Goodrich: Short History of the Chinese People (1943) Vol: I.
3. Translated F. Hirth and W. W. Rockhill. (St. Petersbourg) 1911. Renaud: Relations des Voyages, Vol. I pp.63-64, tells of the massacre of 120,000 foreign merchants, including Arabs and Persians, in Canton during the Hwang-Chao rebellion in 879 A. D.
4. Victor Purcell: The Chinese in Malaya. (London.) 1948. p. 7.

in the Nan Yang is enough to explain their continued overwhelming preponderance.

Nevertheless, despite economic stress and the hope of gain, emigration was by no means an easy business. Up till at least 1860[1] any Chinese who left the Middle Kingdom was committing a capital offence, and until a much later date than this the Chinese government still had no official representatives abroad. The Chinese who ventured overseas did so at their own risk, and with no official protection from their own government were forced to rely upon themselves and their own powers of organisation to protect their own interests. Herein lies a major reason for the development of Associations and Secret Societies.[3]

To the legal difficulties were added physical dangers. Travel by junk in the old days was not a pleasant experience. The voyage from Amoy to Singapore took between 20 and 30 days, in conditions reminiscent of the West African Slave Trade. In 1822 an Amoy junk of eight or nine hundred tons was wrecked on its way to Batavia. The English Lieutenant who went to her rescue stated that there were on board "at the least calculation ... one thousand six hundred persons, from the ages of seventy to six years."[4] On these floating hells scurvy was rife and the death rate high.[5] An informant in Sarawak described his arrival in 1904: too weak to walk.[6] Even to-day fourth class passengers on the China run often have to exist in overcrowding and squalor which would probably kill the average European.

Arrived in his strange new land the immigrant found himself facing strange new difficulties. Tropical climate, virgin jungle and head-hunting Dayaks: the Sinkheh[7] was used to none of them. Sickness contracted on the voyage was cured only slowly in the sticky climate where food was often so scarce that the Rajah's government had to supply rations; after six months an immigrant might taste his first vegetables, his own first crop. A few rough atap houses

---

1. Strictly, until 1894. The principle that Chinese proceeding overseas were committing a crime was disposed of in treaties with foreign powers by 1860, but the law was not actually repealed until 1894. For details of how the Imperial government was eventually brought to recognize the right to emigrate see H.F. MacNair: The Chinese Abroad. (Shanghai) 1925. Chapter 1. As Purcell points out, however, the law could not be enforced. There is a single record of the decapitation of a returned emigrant.
2. The first Chinese Embassy was opened in London in 1874.
3. See also J.J.M. de Groot: Het Kongsiwezen van Borneo. 1885.
4. Quoted in H.F. MacNair: The Chinese Abroad. (Shanghai) 1924. p.33 footnote, from Chinese Repository vol:VI 149-153. MacNair adds:"The editorial comment is in itself enlightening: 'We do not suppose that the Chinese government will do anything to requite those who have saved such of its subjects as have been so undutiful as to leave their country'." The rescue cost Lieut. Pearl £11,000.
5. Of relevant interest are the following figures for the trans-Pacific passage in European ships between the years 1850 and 1856. This voyage was, of course, longer than that to the Nan Yang, but conditions on the junks were probably even worse:

Year	Destination	No. of passengers	No.of boats	No.of dead	Percentage
1850	Peru	740	2	247	33%
1852	Panama	300	1	72	24%
1852	British Guiana	811	3	164	20%
1853	Cuba	700	2	104	15%
1853	Panama	425	1	96	23%
1854	Peru	325	1	47	14%
1856	Peru	332	1	128	39%
1856	Peru	298	1	132	45%

On at least 9 occasions between 1850 and 1872 the coolie passengers are known to have mutinied. H.B. Morse: The International Relations of the Chinese Empire. (London.) 1918. Vol.II pp.170-172, 178.
6. His compatriots put this down to his failure to take a sufficient number of cold shower baths each day. It took him three months to recover.
7. Sinkheh -'new guest'- is a Hokkien term used colloquially in English as well as Chinese to refer to new immigrants.

were the only dwellings.[1] Immigrants usually arrived only with the clothes they stood up in; some had a few dollars besides. Tools of any kind were wanting; a single bowl had to suffice for washing, cooking, carrying water. The jungle was something that no Chinese at first knew how to tackle.The earliest clearings had to be made with the help of Dayak labour, though the 'head-hunting Dayaks' were an object of terror to the Chinese. Again, the difference of language remained a continual source of misunderstanding and annoyance.Always poor, often sick, the Chinese pioneers in Sarawak, as elsewhere in the Nan Yang, yet managed to make their tools, clear the jungle, plant their crops, build their houses, open their shops, and even send their children to school. That they were able to do all this is a great tribute to their toughness, their tenacity and their powers of organisation. Individuals alone could not have survived: but the Chinese immigrants were saved by their extraordinary capacity for mutual help.

For the individual, once settled in, there were two possible ways of advance: he must in any case accumulate some capital, but he could do this either through sheer hard work and saving, or by a stroke of good luck. Good luck stories are not few. Here is one example.

A Sinkheh in Singapore in the early days found a job as watchman to a European firm in one of whose storehouses lay a large quantity of uncured skins. Left to themselves the skins rapidly began to deteriorate, and shortly after his appointment the Chinese watchman was told, by signs, to take the stuff away and dump it in the sea. He took the stuff away, borrowed a small boat, rowed out to a nearby island and patiently washed and scrubbed every skin with salt water. Then he took the now nicely cleaned leather back to his employer. The promotion which followed quickly upon that employer's amazement was the first step in a successful Towkay's[2] career.

Hard work and saving were the more common methods of advance, however, and these took time. A successful business man in Batavia described his early life as one of almost continuous toil. As a child he had been apprenticed to a hard master in China. Grinding beans, fetching and carrying, looking after the young master, took all his energies until he was unable to tell whether the moisture that streamed down his face in the grinding room was sweat or tears or bean curd. In the end he ran away, finding a friend in an older man emigrating to the Dutch Indies who offered to pay his passage in return for his promise to work. Having arrived in Batavia with four and a half dollars in his pocket he found himself worked almost as hard by the new master as by the old one. He stayed in this first job, as a shop assistant, working by day and studying by night, until he was between 40 and 50 years old, by which time he had managed to save 1,000 guilders. His friends urged him to set up on his own, but he decided that he still did not know enough about business methods and feared to risk his money. He therefore left the shop and entered a bigger establishment where he started again from the very bottom, working his way up and learning every aspect of the trade during the next thirteen years. With his own business at last, he became also a leader in the Chinese community, prosperity and prestige increasing together. As he said himself: it is easy enough to talk of a poor man becoming rich, but that small word "becoming", said in less than a second, stands for years and years of bitter struggle.

Shop keeping was one way to success. Agriculture, industry and mining were the others. Virgin land acquired from government could be worked rent free for three years. This would give time for the preliminary clearing and the gathering of the first harvests. Pepper, which had been the main source of Brunei revenues throughout the eighteenth century had gone out of cultivation by 1850, but in 1878 the Second Rajah of Sarawak allocated land to certain Chinese merchants for the development of pepper gardens, and by 1907 Sarawak

---

1. Sibu boasted 30 such huts in 1884. The living conditions of the Chinese refugees from Dutch West Borneo were vividly described by contemporary observers.

2. 'Towkay' - in origin a Hokkien term - is used throughout Malaya and Sarawak to denote the (usually Chinese) head of a firm or shop.

had an annual export of over 5,000 tons. Rubber, which has now replaced pepper as the country's major agricultural export, was first planted in Sarawak in 1900. Here too the main development has been in the hands of Chinese.

The earliest and most important of Chinese industrial activities in Sarawak was the development of sago refineries in Kuching around 1850. Sago flour, which had previously been exported in the unrefined wet state direct to Singapore, was thereafter exported as dry flour. Chinese merchants have monopolized this trade ever since. Mining, for gold, antimony and other metals offered more speculative opportunities. Before the establishment of European control gold miners obtained permission to prospect from the local Sultans. An individual or a company (usually the latter) could then go ahead. Later comers might have to pay these original prospectors for the privilege of working. In a rather similar way an enterprising individual or company might obtain from the Sultan permission to open up a certain district. The procedure was the same as that followed by European Joint Stock Companies when setting up their factories. The territory so granted formed a little imperium of its own within which the grantee had full rights, including the right to levy what charges he pleased.

Once European government had been established there were other avenues open to able and intelligent men. The clerks in government service obtained only their fixed salaries, but under the Dutch government, at least, the leaders of the Chinese community, the Kapitans China and others, who were entrusted with the task of collecting taxes from their compatriots received a "commission" of 8% on their takings. Most lucrative of all were the various "farms" (monopoly concessions) granted by all European governments in the East Indies. In Sarawak, for example, there were "farms" over opium, gambling, arrack and pawnshops. As the administration obtained a large part of its revenue from these sources, so also the enterprising merchant "farmers" were in a position to gain a large income.[1]

Those who made good in one way or another are remembered; far more numerous, and, for the countries of the Nan Yang as a whole, far more important, are the hundreds of thousands of forgotten men, those who died as they lived in poverty, or returned penniless to China.

On one of the last days of November, 1948, a tired, bent old man waited on the wharf at Kuching. Twentyfour years ago in the prime of his life he had arrived in Sarawak; now the Foochow Association was sending him home, an aged pauper. His story has been repeated hundreds, thousands, of times. A mechanic in Foochow, he decided, at the age of 48, to go abroad for a year or two to make his fortune. A cousin in Sibu invited him to come over and paid the $130 for his fare in return for his promise to work and his care of the cousin's wife on the voyage. For five months he worked for the cousin, but being paid barely enough for his food he soon went elsewhere, working first as a labourer on a rubber estate. He stayed there a year, planting rubber for the reward of 4 cents for every 40 plants. The next 13 years he worked on an orange estate, receiving $15 a month and his meals. Then, fifteen years after he had left home ("for a year or two") he was ready to venture into rubber growing on his own account. For $350 he acquired 5 acres of land, and for 3½ years he worked it. Then the Japanese came. Rubber was unsaleable and he was lucky to get rid of his land for $750. He managed to live on this until the liberation, which found him with $50 in his pocket. He tried to get a plot of land to plant vegetables, and for a time he worked as a caretaker on an orange estate where he got $40 a month, and then on a second estate for $18 a month and his food. Seventeen years before, he had run a thorn into his leg. The wound had never healed, and the great running sore on his shin now made him useless even for caretaking. By 1948 nobody would employ him. He was reduced to living on the charity of his friends, sleeping by night in the Chinese version of St. Martin's crypt - the theatre of the local temple. Then the friends went back to China. Completely destitute he turned to the Foochow Association, in Kuching, which gave him 18 cents a day (enough for two meals, one of

1. Cf. F.W. Burbidge: <u>The Gardens of the Sun</u>. (London.) 1880. pp.23, 159. et alii. In the year 1900 the total revenue of the Sarawak government was $915,966, of which $282,535 came from the farming of opium, gaming houses, sales of spirits and pawnshops.

rice and one of porridge) and half his passage back to China. Government paid the other half.

Hard as he had worked this man had found it impossible to save. The cost of living, remitting money to his family in China and gambling had proved too much. In China he had left a wife, a son and daughter-in-law, three grandsons and a granddaughter. Over the twentyfour years of his absence he had sent about $500 home, keeping in touch with his family through about thirty letters, for which he had had to pay a professional letter-writer. Gambling had been his sole form of entertainment, and he gambled heavily, wagering as much as 39-40 dollars (more than a month's pay) at a time. Gambling had also involved him in the two serious quarrels of his life: one with a fellow Foochow whose threat of vengeance had caused him to flee from Sibu to Sarikei, and one with a Malay who had beaten him up badly but who had later been brought to court and, most satisfactorily, fined $65. Now there was not even a chance to gamble any more. His son had been conscripted into the Chinese army. No news had been received from him for two years. His eldest grandson, born the year he had left home, had twice written begging him to return. Now, twenty-four years older and without the longed-for fortune, he was ready to go.

Success comes to a few, failure to many. Neither success nor failure but simple stagnation is the lot of most of the professional people. In 1949 a teacher, who graduated from Senior Middle School, in Chao An, described how he came to Sarawak 16 years before, full of enthusiasm and even idealism. The Nan Yang, he had heard, was fabulously rich,[1] its people eager for learning, his own career assured. For the first year he taught in a Fukien sponsored school in Kuching, but being from Chao An[2] he made no particular friends upon the school board and his appointment was not confirmed. He then went to a rural Hakka school in the First Division and stayed there for some time, but found his enthusiasm and his ideals stultified by the constant threat of insecurity. Every term saw a reshuffling of teachers. The Chinese schools are mostly run by local private school boards. Every teacher finds sooner or later that he has his patrons or friends on the school board, but as all the board members are small local shopkeepers they are also all rivals, and if one is your friend then others are your enemies. As a result the teacher's tenure of his job is remarkably uncertain. At the same time, the boards being small and money being raised by local subscription, the teachers' salaries are even more uncertain. It is not unknown for board members themselves to borrow from their teachers. A teacher must have some savings to fall back on; but if almost every term there is a General Post nearly all his savings go on travelling expenses in the search for new jobs. During the Japanese occupation the Chao An teacher married, and now has three children. His wife also is a working teacher, and the whole family lives in Kuching, where with their combined salaries they can afford a single cubicle in a shop-house. With two adults and three children constantly on top of one another, with heat and noise, and without privacy, relaxation at home is impossible, entertaining out of the question. This man and his wife are teachers but they cannot get books or magazines to improve their minds, and even if they could there would be no place to read them. Teachers are expected to be leaders of the community, but a life of insecurity has quenched their idealism, and fear of losing their jobs makes them chary of political activity. There is the occasional game of mahjong to enliven things: otherwise nothing. Nervously frustrated in teaching this man turned his hand to business during the war, but without success. Now he is

---

1. Returned travellers, and those writing from overseas, tend to boast unduly of their prosperity. Despite the proportion of paupers who are sent back like the old man in the text here, the majority of the unsuccessful never return at all. Villagers at home therefore tend to judge the Nan Yang entirely by the prosperous few who come back to flaunt their success.

2. For the significance of this see below p.13.

thinking of returning to China; but it will be long before he can scrape together enough money for five passages.[1]

The modifications of the traditional Chinese way of life which have appeared in the overseas communities of the Nan Yang would make a fascinating study. In general they are of two kinds: those imposed by the new geographical and economic environment, and those adopted from other, indigenous or alien, cultures. In so far as these are concerned with the organisation of social relationships[2] they form the subject matter of this book: in so far as they apply to material culture and every day life they have yet to be studied in detail. The tropical climate imposes new hygienic measures, which have required cultural recognition; thus every Chinese in the Nan Yang is supposed to rub himself down seven times every day with a small wooden stick, and souse himself with cold water from top to toe: every fortnight he must drink a specially concocted ginseng and chrysanthemum tea to cleanse his bowels. Rice remains the staple diet, but so it is for the indigenous population: Chinese tastes in other kinds of food change before the luxuriance of tropical fruits and the succulence of Malay curries. Clothing, influenced by climate and culture contact, becomes a mixture of Chinese, European and Malay: shorts or trousers and shirts, sarongs, frocks, two-piece pyjama-like garments, rubber-soled slippers are seen everywhere. Housing for the poorer Chinese is mainly of the local type, but the rich often demonstrate their social position by building in the Chinese style.

This last point deserves emphasis. Except amongst the long established Baba families, it is probably true to say that the richer the Nan Yang Chinese the more self-consciously he strives to adhere to a "Chinese" way of life. In many of the material details of everyday life these Nan Yang Chinese often appear more Chinese than the Chinese of China. Amid the alien corn they hark back to Chinese precedents all the more strongly, even tending to conserve what in China itself has been abandoned. A well-to-do Chinese wedding in the Nan Yang brings out replicas of all the old Ming costumes which are seldom seen in China to-day.

It is, of course, the common tendency of "provincial" communities everywhere to be some twenty or thirty years behind the times. The overseas Chinese communities are large, contacts with home fairly easy, the sense of the superiority of Chinese culture almost complete. It is not surprising, then, to find such faithful reproductions of the material background of Chinese life, even if the reproduction is old-fashioned and sometimes ludicrously over-emphasised. When a certain Kongsi house was being built in Sarawak, the pillars, which had been made rectangular after the usual local pattern, had to be taken out and rounded off because "in China they are always circular".

In part this emphasis upon things Chinese is an expression of a great nostalgia for home. However many years they have stayed in the South Seas the China-born Chinese, and many of the overseas born too, keep their eyes fixed on China and their hearts set upon home. A Hainanese saying runs:"The rivers and streams of Hainan go far, far away to the oceans, but they always return at the last". Dreaming of his future the Chinese emigrant sees himself back in his own village giving a three days' theatrical performance at the village temple, with a great banquet and hundreds of fire-crackers, buying more land, building a fine new house, perhaps engaging a beautiful concubine to care for

---

1. The actual sale of children is by no means an unusual procedure even in the overseas Chinese communities. On one occasion when the writer was engaged in conversation in a certain shop in Kuching, it transpired that no less than three of the adults present had been forced by poverty to dispose of their children in this way. One, a woman customer from the rural districts, had sold two of her five children; a boy for $160 and a girl for $100. An assistant in the store, whose salary was $80 a month, had sold his middle son, a sickly and therefore expensive boy, for $100. A tailor's employee, also working in the same building at a wage of $65 per month, had sold the youngest of his three sons for $200. No one expressed surprise at this state of affairs.

2. Apart, that is, from family relationships with which this volume is not directly concerned.

his declining years. Sometimes the dream comes true: the temple ceremonies
are performed, the banquet eaten, the crackers fired off. Sometimes the concubine is engaged, the house built, the land bought - and from the land the
newly dispossessed in their turn are driven overseas to seek their fortunes
too. The circle is complete. The stream continues to flow far, far away -
but only a few drops ever really return at the last.

III

W A R P   A N D   W O O F   O F   C H I N E S E   A S S O C I A T I O N S

When a Chinese leaves his homeland and comes to this part of the world,
he tends to mix with those whose speech he can understand, to travel with
them and stay at hotels owned by them. He tends to serve his apprenticeship
in his new country in the occupation in which a majority of his own dialect
speakers are found, and having served his apprenticeship he tends to stay in
the same trade all his life. When he opens a business he seeks a partner of
the same dialect group, and employs his assistants likewise. He likes to
marry a girl who speaks his dialect, and when he dies he is carried to the
cemetery where others who spoke as he did already lie burried. All this is
well-known. What is more difficult to see is the institutional framework upon which these social phenomena are based. In other words, what is the organisation of these dialect groups? How are they actually constituted?

The only easily visible organisation in the Chinese community is that of
the "association" or "guild". But these terms as commonly used refer to
nothing more than a sort of club building at which members can read the newspapers or play mahjong. The building usually contains a hall for meetings
and a room with an altar for religious purposes. The Chinese in foreign lands
have 3,940 such organisations, of which 886 are described as "professional organisations", 938 as "patriotic societies" and 2,116 as "permanent social organisations".[1] About 900 of these are in Singapore;[2] in Sarawak 156.[3] There
are so many associations of this kind everywhere in the Nan Yang that it has
even been suggested that they are partly responsible for the notorious over-
crowding in the cities.

The existence of so many organised associations in the overseas Chinese
communities points to the existence of numerous social groups, but the real
nature of these groups cannot be discovered from a mere survey of these organisations. In British territories in South East Asia all associations, societies, clubs, companies and limited companies with more than ten members[4]
are required to notify the Government of their existence. It was from the
official lists of such associations that the above figures were taken, but obviously the lumping together of almost every kind of organised social group
in this way is of little sociological significance. Some of the associations
whose names appear on the lists are defunct, others are very small; some are
simply recreational clubs, others are organisations of business men. We are
not concerned with these, but with the larger associations which comprise
members from the same dialect group, the same locality in China or the same
clan.

Whether or not any particular listed association is of structural significance can only be discovered by inspection of its membership and its actual
functions, as opposed to its professed aims. Many associations which profess
to be merely recreational or educational or professional may be described as

1. According to an investigation made at the end of 1944, and published in
   The China Handbook 1937-1945 (Chinese Ministry of Information), (MacMillan,
   New York), 1947, p.32.
2. Directory of Chinese Schools and Associations in Singapore (in Chinese).
3. Sarawak Government Gazette. October 1st, 1947.
4. Before the Japanese war this list included Trade Unions.

dialect associations in the sense that they tend to draw their membership from the same dialect groups. In practice a small but useful distinction can be made between the small association with comparatively limited aims (e.g. The Teachers' Association, the Overseas Youth Associations, various School alumni assocations etc., etc.)[1] and the larger dialect associations (based on locality, clan or occupation) whose aims are summed up in the official lists as "social and charitable". These latter may be described as organisations for the promotion of group solidarity and mutual help. Both are, of course, associations, that is groups voluntarily organised for the promotion of a certain end or ends, but the former type we shall call "Clubs" and the latter "Associations" with an upper case initial.

It is important to recognise that an Association as listed is merely that portion of the Chinese group structure which has officially notified government of its existence. Without this notification the set of relationships comprised in the Association would still exist; a group of people from the same locality could co-operate together just as effectively without incorporation on the official lists. In actual fact the listed membership of a dialect (locality, clan or occupational) Association is usually small, a few hundreds at the most, while the numbers in a dialect group as a whole may run into tens, or hundreds, of thousands. The links between listed members and eligible non-members vary in strength and may be complex in nature. If we are to understand the organisation of the different social groups which compose an overseas Chinese community we cannot do better than begin with the most conspicuous institutions, the listed Associations, and by setting out the complicated patterns of functions and relationships involved in these, we shall find that we are led into a discussion of the actual constitution of dialect, locality, clan and occupational groups.

As Appendix III shows there are ten main dialect groups in Kuching, but none of these can be connected with one particular Chinese province, because linguistic and adminstrative boundaries in China do not necessarily coincide. Even the people concerned often find it difficulty to draw hard and fast lines of division between one dialect group and another, and when a definite classification is finally made it is not always easy to justify it. For example, as Foochow is the capital of the province of Fukien one would expect to find whose who speak the Foochow dialect classified as Fukienese; in actual fact, however, a Foochow-speaking person is always considered separately and under the heading "Fukien" are placed only those who speak the southern Fukien dialect - Amoy. The situation of the Cantonese people is similar. Under the regional grouping "Cantonese" should be included Teochows, Hakkas and people from the Luichow peninsula and Hainan island, but in fact only those from the central part of Kwangtung province who speak the Cantonese dialect proper are counted as such.

The following is a list of the different Chinese dialect groups in Sarawak:

1. The Foochow Group[2]. The Foochow dialect is spoken in Foochow, which is the capital of the province of Fukien. Closely similar dialects are spoken in all the hsien near Foochow, including Changlo, Futsing, Fuan, Futing,

---

1. Associations of this type often comprise a mixture of dialects.

2. In order avoid the confusion which would result from employing different dialect forms, most of the Chinese names in this study are recorded in Mandarin, and the Wade system of Romanization, as the most widely known system, is used. Where the Mandarin form of pronunciation is so markedly different as to be misleading, or where the dialect pronunciation is commonly accepted even by Mandarin speakers it is retained. For instance Hakka is used instead of Khehchia (kheh), Teochow instead of Ch'aochow, Chao An instead of Chanan. For details of population numbers see Appendix III below.

Lienking, Loynan, Pingnan and Kutien.[1]

In Sarawak Foochow people form the second most numerous Chinese dialect group[2]. In the Third Division they are undoubtedly in the majority[3] especially in Binatang, Sarikei, Sebauh and Payut, and indeed the town of Sibu is known both in Sarawak and in China as "New Foochow". In Sibu Foochow speakers are found in every occupation. In Kuching and the First Division they are barbers, and coffee-shop keepers, but are mostly to be found in the building trade: most of the masons and the carpenters employed in building are Foochow speaking, as are all the eight big contractors. There are separate Foochow Associations in Kuching and Sibu.

2. The Henghua Group. This dialect is spoken by the people of Henghua hsien and Sienya hsien in Fukien. Most of the Henghua people in Sarawak come from just two groups of villages, and bear the same half dozen or so surnames. Henghua people are also to be found in Sandakan, in Tawan in North Borneo and in Malacca. In Kuching 96% of the fishermen are from this group, their boats (of which there are 269) being distinguished from the local Malay craft by their straight keel plates. Henghua people also account for the overwhelming majority of the bicycle shop workers in Sarawak (84% in Kuching). In order to organise a system of mutual help among Henghua fisherman the Kotak (or Fishing Boat) Association has been formed. Each time a boat goes out its members contribute $1 to the common fund which stands as an insurance against possible disaster.[4] The Kotak Association is affiliated to the Henghua dialect Association, sharing the same building and the same staff, and many of the Henghua people in Kuching are members of both Associations.

The Kotak Association deals with disputes at sea, loss of nets, and so on; the Henghua Association handles domestic and other disputes ashore.

3. The Fukien Group (Amoy or Minan group). This group covers the dialect spoken in the Southern part of Fukien province, that is: Amoy, Kinmin, Tungan, Anki, Hanan, Yungchan, Tehwa, Haicheng, Lungyen, Lungki, Changpu, Nantsing, Huan, Changtai, Yunshiao, Changpui and so on. This is the dialect often referred to as Hokkien.

In Sarawak members of this group have generally been identified with the export trade, but in actual fact they have also penetrated into almost every occupation and thus it is rather difficult to identify them with any particular one. They are, next to the Teochows, the second most

---

1. In Fukien province the differences in dialects seem to be more pronounced than elsewhere. Each separate hsien may have its own peculiar dialect, quite distinct from that of its neighbours. Among the oversea Chinese these minor differences in dialect tend to disappear, and a new dialect, somewhat different from any to be found inside China appears. This new dialect includes a great number of new words and expressions. For instance: in Kuching the English expression "I say" has been widely adopted as an exclamation, even by people who have no other knowledge of the English language. In the counting of large sums, too, the Chinese method is being superseded by the English, and the Chinese term "wan", meaning ten-thousand, is thus being superseded by the use of terms which exactly translate the English ten thousand, eleven thousand etc. A large number of words in pidgin-English have also been added to the local vocabulary, for example: "hua" for warrant, "puu" for protest, "gglan" for grant.

2. The most numerous is the Hakka group.

3. Total Chinese in Third Division: 58,899. Foochow: 38,887. (Census Report 1947).

4. It is often considered that in the last few years, especially during the Japanese occupation, fishermen have been able to make a fortune. But most of these Henghua people remain very poor, their village still being the worst slum area of Kuching, although their Better Living Co-operative Society has the largest capital of any Co-operative in Sarawak.

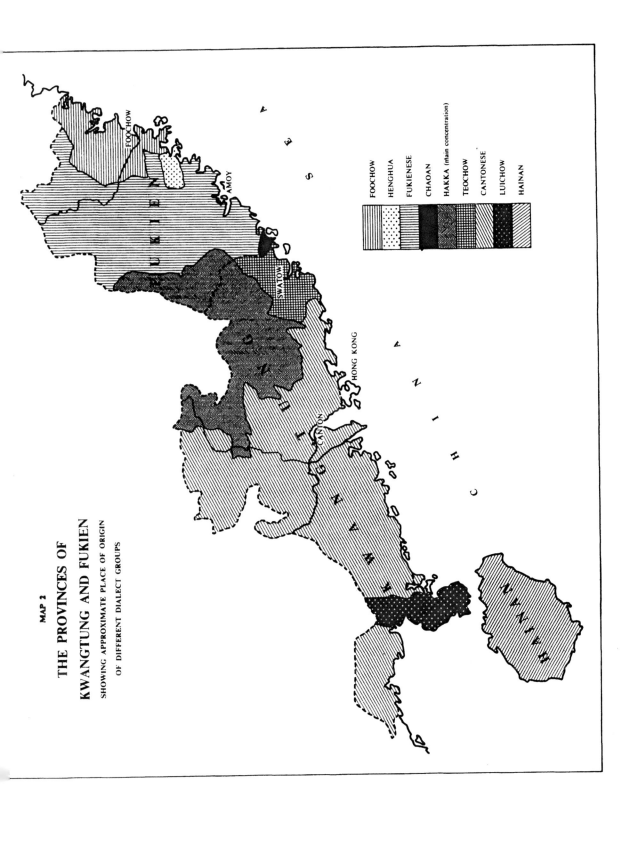

MAP 2

THE PROVINCES OF KWANGTUNG AND FUKIEN

SHOWING APPROXIMATE PLACE OF ORIGIN
OF DIFFERENT DIALECT GROUPS

FOOCHOW
HENGHUA
FUKIENESE
CHAOAN
HAKKA (main concentration)
TEOCHOW
CANTONESE
LUICHOW
HAINAN

numerous group in the grocery business, and they dominate the miscellaneous goods stores. They also occupy a very strong position in goldsmithing and as agents through whom money is remitted to China. In the last resort, as we shall see later, the major part of the export trade from Kuching is controlled by a single Fukienese. Thus, although fewer in numbers than the Teochow group, the Fukienese occupy an equally or even more important position. This is true not only of Sarawak, but throughout the Nan Yang, except perhaps in Siam.

Besides Kuching the places where Fukienese dominate, either in number or in financial strength, are Lingga, Pusa, Lawas, Limbong, Baram, Mukah, Kapit, Kanowwit. The headquarters of the Fukien Association is in Kuching. There is also the Nan Kiaw Club, a recreational club, whose members are mainly Fukienese.

4. The Chanan (Chao An)[1] Group. The Sarawak Census Report (1947) includes this group, which consists of immigrants from Chao An hsien, with the Fukien dialect group. According to strict linguistic classification this is probably correct. On the other hand Chao An hsien is geographically near to the Teochow speaking groups in China, and its dialect may be regarded as in several respects mid-way between Teochow and Fukienese. Moreover, for historical reasons, the Chao An people both in Kuching and the out-stations have occupied a distinctive position which justifies their being classed separately here. About sixty years ago the biggest financial power in the Colony was a Chao An-speaking Chinese named T'ien (Ch'an). Through his influence a large number of his clansmen and neighbours were brought to Sarawak, and with their help much of the early work in opening up the outstations for the collection of rubber and other local products was done. Since then the power of the Ch'an clan has gradually dwindled, but in many small places, like Dalat, Balingian, Daro, Niah, Sibuti, Matu, Balawai, Tatau and Maludam, Chao An people still maintain an important position in the commercial field.

Before the Japanese war nearly all the wharf labourers in Kuching were of Chao An origin, and they are still very largely so. They also supply quite a number of masons and carpenters for the Kuching contractors, of whom many (nearly 29) speak this dialect.

There is a special Chao An Association, distinct from either Fukien or Teochow, with its headquarters in Kuching. There are also two Chao An clans,[2] T'ien (Ch'an) and Shen (Sim), which have formed their own registered Associations.

5. The Ch'aochow (Teochow) Group. The Teochow dialect is spoken in the eastern part of Kwangtung province, including the following hsien: Ch'aoao, Ch'aoyang, Swatow, Fengshun, Kityang, Funing, Hweilai, Chenghai, Nanao and Jaoping.

From Siam, where they form the greatest proportion of the Chinese population, southwards, Teochow speaking people dominate the grocery trade, selling such provisions as rice, salted fish, vegetables, fruit and condiments of all kinds. Most of these foodstuffs are the produce of southern Kwangtung, exported from Swatow and the re-exported from Singapore. Kuching is no exception to this identification of Teochows with the grocery trade. Concentrated mainly in the Gambier Road Teochow people run more than 38% of the grocery shops in Kuching, and people of other dialect groups certainly regard them as the most efficient merchants. Most of the Teochow speaking people in Sarawak are urban dwellers, but in Simanggang, Debak, Betong and Bintulu there are a good many Teochow farmers.

The Teochow Associations' building in Kuching also houses the Ch'aoch'ao (Teoteo) Overseas Club, a recreational club for Teochow speaking members. Many Teochow people are also members of the Grocery Association, which is dominated by Teochows, and the Union Merchants' Association,

---

1. For this and the Ch'aochow group the local pronunciation (Chao An and Teochow) is retained here on account of its far greater familiarity in the Nan Yang.
2. See Chapter V below.

whose leadership is primarily Fukienese.

6. The Cantonese Group.   Cantonese is not spoken by all the people of Kwangtung province, but only in the central districts, mainly in the Hsiens near Canton city and Macao, Hweiyang (Hweichou) and Kaoyao (Chaoching), and in Hong Kong.

Though they are numerous in the Third and Fifth Divisions the Cantonese occupy a rather minor position in Kuching. Like the Fukienese they have penetrated into almost every kind of occupation, but apart from their complete command of the watch and clock trade it seems that they have not attained an important position in any of them.   One of the two Chinese commercial banks in Kuching is a branch of the Cantonese owned Kwangli bank in Singapore, but this does not imply any marked Cantonese dominance in general commerce.   The Cantonese connection with mining is noticeable in Sarawak as in Malaya, though many of the Cantonese labourers in Miri (Fifth Division) only went there after the failure of their venture into pepper farming in the Third Division.

The Cantonese Association is in Kuching.

7. The Luichow Group.   This dialect is spoken in the Luichow peninsula.

In Sarawak this is a small group, mostly engaged in labouring work in the outstations, in the sago factories and rubber gardens.   There are only eleven Luichow families in the bazaar area of Kuching, and the only shop that has ever been run by a Luichow speaking man is a coffee shop. It is generally agreed that the making of charcoal is the occupation peculiar to Luichow people, and, as we shall see later, this is true of the actual workers, though only six of the eleven charcoal making businesses are Luichow owned.

The Luichow Association in Kuching, having no suitably qualified member, is compelled to employ someone from another dialect group as secretary.

8. The Hainan (Hailam) Group.   The Hainan dialect is spoken on the island of that name.

This is the group which is outstandingly associated with the coffee shop business in Sarawak, and also with the occupations of cooks and sailors in European and Chinese employment.   The general opinion of the overseas Chinese is that Hainan people are both energetic and emotionally volatile.

At the present time, in addition to the ordinary Hainan dialect Association there are three Associations with which Hainanese are particularly connected.   These are occupational Associations: the Coffee Employees' Association and the Nyap Jee Club which is predominantly for the cooks working in European households.

9. The Hakka (Kheh) Group.   This is the largest group of Chinese in Sarawak, especially in the First Division.   Their origin, history and distribution, are discussed in Appendix II.

Originally Hakka people from different parts of Kwangtung province formed separate Associations.   Thus there was the P'u-i Association for those from Tap'u Hsien, and the Kiaying Hakka Association for those from the Kiaying prefecture, consisting of the five hsiens Mei, Chiaoling, Wuhua, Hsingning, Pingyuan.   Later a (general) Hakka Association was set up. The two smaller Associations continued in existence, though without very much raison d'être, since most of the work concerning the Hakka people was taken over by the general Association.

10. Southern Mandarin Group (Kweilin Kuan-Hua Group).   This includes all Chinese from other parts of China who speak some variety of Mandarin.[1]

1. In common parlance among the oversea Chinese the people of China are divided into three groups: the Cantonese, the Fukienese and the people of Shanghai, the last sometimes called San Kiang Jen, that is people of the three 'Kiang' provinces, Kiangsi, Kiangsu and Chekiang. This last category has been widely used to cover all those overseas Chinese who speak other dialects, especially Mandarin.

In Kuching most of these people are from the provinces of Kiangsi and Anwhei. The Anwhei people are mostly engaged in the stationery trade,and as pedlars selling spectacles and so forth. People from Hupei are considered to be identified with the fashionable occupation of tooth-artistry,[1] though in actual fact the identification is not complete. Kiangsi people are exclusively engaged in furniture making; all the furniture making establishments in Kuching are either owned by, or employ, members of this group, all of whom come from a single small town, Shih-Tan-K'ai, in Fa-Chen hsien.

There are no special Associations for this somewhat miscellaneous group. If they desire or need Association membership, Mandarin speakers can join with any other dialect group. For example, Kiangsi people often join the Hakka Association, and some of the Hupei people have joined the Cantonese Association.[2]

This classification, which is based upon similarity of dialect and geographical proximity, is a very flexible one. Because people from the same district do not always speak the same dialect a great number of overlapping cases can always be found. This is especially so in Kwangtung, where three different dialects - Teochow, Cantonese and Hakka - exist side by side. It is very difficult to tell which group a person from, say, Hweiyang, belongs to until he opens his mouth to speak. Quite a number of disputes have occurred among the various dialect Associations in Kuching about the criteria of membership, especially in matters involving expenditure; for example a dispute may arise in this way when it is a question of giving financial assistance to a person from a certain district who wishes to return to China. Generally speaking, however, dialect and locality are so closely linked that one might just as well talk of "territorial" as "dialect" Associations.

This is made quite clear by the naming system followed by these Associations. Each dialect group in Kuching which forms its own Association names it either after the dialect itself or after the district of origin in China. These place names, however, always refer to a much wider area than that from which all the members actually come, and in fact the original geographical scatter of the members may often be narrowed down to a single hsien, although the name of their Association may refer to an area containing many hsien. Material gathered in Kuching from the registration cards of all the Associations which are organised on a territorial basis makes it quite clear that in each there is a dominant group of members who come from an even more restricted area. Thus in those Associations which are composed of dialect groups inhabiting only a single hsien the dominant groups come always from a single division of the hsien, or even from a single village. This is clearly illus-

---

1. Not, strictly speaking, dentists. They are mainly engaged in inserting decorative gold fillings. They also pull teeth.

2. These ten groups can be re-classified according to provinces as follows :

(i) Fukien province:	(ii) Kwangtung province:	(iii) Other provinces
Foochow group	Cantonese group	Southern
Henghua "	Teochow "	Mandarin
Chao An "	Hainan "	group
Fukien "	Luichow "	
Hakka "	Hakka "	

A classification by linguistic affinity can also be made, as follows :

(i) Fukien branch	(ii) Cantonese branch	(iii) Mandarin Branch
Foochow group	Hakka group	Southern
Henghua "	Cantonese group	Mandarin
Chao An "		group
Fukien "		
Teochow "		
Hainan "		
Luichow "		

trated by the figures collected from three of these small Associations in Kuching :

T A B L E   2

DOMINANT GROUPS IN THREE SMALL CHINESE ASSOCIATIONS IN KUCHING

Name of Association	Total Membership	Dominant group	Membership of dominant group	Percentage of total membership
Henghua	314	From Hout'un & Kiangshia villages	252	80·2%
Chao An	299	From the first division of Chao An hsien	144	48%
Tap'u (Tappu) (Hakka)	269	From P'eihou village	138	51·3%

Table 3 shows that a similar state of affairs exists in the larger Associations. The following eight dialect Associations draw their members from
anything between four and thirty-two different hsiens in China, yet in each
those from a particular hsien or hsiens are predominant.

T A B L E   3

DOMINANT GROUPS AMONG THE CHINESE ASSOCIATIONS IN KUCHING

Name of Dialect Association	No.of hsien in China in which the Dialect is spoken	Total Membership of Dialect Association in Kuching	Place of Origin of Dominant Group	Membership of Dominant Group	Percentage of the total Membership
Teochow	8	387	Ch'ao An hsien	340	87·6%
Luichow	4	198	Suikai hsien	134	67.6%
Kaying (Hakka)	5	93	Mei hsien	80	64·5%
Fukien	21	286	Kinmin, Tungan, Szumin, Haicheng hsien	192	61·2%
Hainan	10	514	Wench'ang hsien	262	50·9%
Hakka	13	569	Hoppu (5th Division of Kityang hsien)	277	48·8%
Kwong Hwee Seow (Cantonese)	32	2389	Taishan, Sinwin, Kaiping Enping hsien	1099	46%
Foochow	6	253	Changlo hsien	81	32%

These two tables show also the way in which all the members of a single Association share a closely similar geographical origin in China. A Chinese who comes as an immigrant to join an already existing community of overseas Chinese makes his first contacts with others who not only speak his own dialect, as is well known, but also come from his own locality, often his own home town or village. This kind of shared experience is especially significant for those who feel themselves exiles in a foreign land and the closer the original geographical proximity the more intense the sentiments of mutual sympathy are likely to be.[1]

In addition to this, the different Associations are subject to a third very strong binding force: the bond of clanship. Many of the co-members of a Chinese Associations overseas are members of the same clan, that is, they bear the same surname and are attached to one another by genealogical relationships. Indeed, this intricate system of clanship should be considered as the fundamental basis on which the social relations of the overseas Chinese are regulated, and by which the sense of mutual solidarity is made very real. This is especially true of the rural districts.[2]

Clan relationships are exemplified most conspicuously in the dominant groups of each Association, which usually comprise one big clan. If we can call the dominant group the prop on which the Association as a whole is supported, then the dominant clan is the foundation in which the prop is set. In the following table an investigation into the dominant groups of certain Associations is made. It is interesting to note that the smaller the Association the more power is held by a single clan.

All the figures in Table 3A come from the names of members as they are recorded on the Associations' registration cards. This, of course, does not account for all the members of all Associations, nevertheless the Table does present a fair picture of the intricacy of clanship relations among Association members. The actual situation is even more complicated than appears here, for although each clan only covers a small section of the members of each Association, yet through matrimonial (affinal) relationships genealogical ties can be traced very widely indeed. An Association is, therefore, not merely an organisation which expresses the provincial feelings of its members, it is also the expression of quite other types of social relationships (i.e. clanship) which do not at all appear in its title.

Whenever the overseas Chinese are being considered, attention must always be turned to questions of economic significance. If we consider the actual activities of the various dialect Associations we can see at once that, without exception, their most important function is in connection not with dialect, locality or clan matters, as such, but with the economic interests of the occupation which is followed by the majority of its members. With the exception of Teochows and Fukienese, nearly all the members of each dialect group in Kuching are engaged in the single occupation peculiar to their group. Hainan people, for example, are mostly engaged in the coffee shop business, Henghua people are predominantly fishermen and bicycle dealers, all the tinsmiths are Hakkas from Tap'u hsien, and all the carpenters come from a single small town in Fengch'ing hsien in Kiangsi province. This close identification of a particular dialect group with a particular job, which is described in detail in Chapter IX below means that the various dialect Associations have a definite economic raison d'être, and conversely the various occupational Associations, where they exist, are either substitutes for, or subsidiary to,

---

1. Certain villages in Fukien and Kwangtung are famed as "overseas villages", because so many of their inhabitants have emigrated. Cp. Chen Ta: Emigrant communities in South China. (O.U.P.) 1939. In Fukien province three such villages are Sse-Hsi, in Ching-Chiang hsien, Hsi-Shan, in Nan-An hsien and Ch'u-Yang, in Hai-Ch'eng hsien. From these come nearly all the leading Fukienese families in the Nan Yang.

2. Cp. Chapter V below.

T A B L E   3A

DOMINANT CLANS OF DOMINANT GROUPS OF CHINESE ASSOCIATIONS IN KUCHING

Dominant group	Dominant clans of Dominant group		No. of people in each clan	Percentage of the total membership of the Dominant group
	Pronounced in : Mandarin / Dialect			
Hout'un,Kiangshia & Pinghai village (Dominant group of Henghua Association)	Chen* Cheng* Ho* Kuo* Chang* Fang* Cho*	Tan Tin Ho Koah Tiu^n Png Toh	58) 38) 19) 14) 209 15) 13) 12)	89·3
First Division of Chao An Hsien (Dominant group of Chao An Association)	T'ien* Shen Chen	Chan Sim Tan	43) 41) 99 15)	68·7
P'eihou and neighbouring villages (dominant group of Pu-i Hakka Association)	Yang* Hsiao*	Yong Sian	70) 87 17)	63
Ch'ao An Hsien (Dominant group of Teochow Association)	Chen* Shen* Chang* Lu* Hsu* Kuo*	Tan Sim Tiu^n Law Kho Koah	62) 51) 30) 208 30) 14) 20)	61·1
Suik'ai Hsien (Dominant group of Luichow Association)	Chen* Shih*	Tan Chia	49) 66 17)	33·3
Mei Hsien (Dominant group of Kaying Hakka Association)	Liang	Liong	17	28·3
Wench'ang Hsien (Dominant group of Hainan Association)	Chang*	Tiu^n	63	24
Hoppu Division (Dominant group of General Hakka Association)	T'sai*	Chhoa	59	21·3

* All members of this clan originate from the same village in China.

particular dialect Associations.[1]

The various dialect, locality and clan Associations are the outward and visible signs of the social structure of an overseas Chinese community. As we have seen there is no way of differentiating sharply between Associations based upon shared dialect, shared locality, shared clanship, or even, as a rule, shared occupation. All these primary social relationships tend to overlap, so that many of the members of an Association organised on the basis, say, of locality, may be expected to be related also by clanship, and most of them will also share the same occupation. Obviously, too, they will be speakers of the same dialect. Thus to classify a Chinese association according to its name alone is always misleading. For instance, the Nyap Yee Club in Kuching has a title which may be translated simply as "Recreational Club"; actually, however, it is, as we have seen, an Association organised on an occupation-cum-dialect basis, all the members being Hainan speaking cooks and domestic servants in European employ, most of them coming from contiguous districts in Hainan island and many of them linked by clanship. An Association like this thus comprises a cluster of social relationships, usually embracing all the most significant aspects of Chinese social life. The widest, and the most conspicuous, of these is dialect similarity. To the individual inside it, the Chinese community appears a more or less self-contained universe, within which the dialect groups are the main divisions and the Associations which are linked with dialect differences the major institutions; but the observer can see the dialect relationships shot through with strands of neighbourhood, of clanship, and of occupational identification.

IV

THE NATURE OF THE CHINESE COMMUNITY

The clustering of a number of conceptually different social relationships which is demonstrated in the dialect Associations in Kuching is common to all overseas Chinese communities. The close link between dialect and place of origin which was described in the preceding chapter is too obvious to require emphasis. The operations of clanship and occupational grouping are less evident and understanding of the structure of the Chinese community demands their fuller analysis. The registered Associations themselves are not the most suitable field for such an analysis, however, partly because of the great difficulty of disentangling the various social relationships which are to be found together in them, and partly because they are by no means fully representative of the whole Chinese community. The Associations give us the key to the fundamental relationships of overseas Chinese social structure, but in order to see how they work we must look to the wider Chinese community.

First, however, some popular misconceptions must be removed. It is a common custom in everyday speech to lump all the Chinese in a given South East Asian community together without considering variations within the group. If one is thinking solely in terms of a racial or cultural unit it is quite legitimate to consider "the Chinese" as one, but any study of Chinese social structure necessarily demands more detailed analysis. We have already mentioned the major divisions into dialect groups. These are well-known. What are less obvious are the economic cleavages within the Chinese community.

The familiar habit of referring to all the overseas Chinese together as, say, "shopkeepers" or "laundrymen" is obviously not intended to be taken seriously, but there is another more important sense in which the Chinese are thought of as occupying a single economic position. Thus it is frequently stated that the societies of South East Asia are "plural" in form, and this notion carries with it the implication that different racial, or cultural,

---

1. Tables 11,12 pp.48,49,51 show the close relationship between each dialect group and its affiliated occupation, whether or not this occupational group has been organised as an Association.

groups are identified with distinct economic statuses:at the bottom a "native" economy based mainly upon labour, at the top a "European" economy based upon large-scale enterprise capital, and in the middle a "Chinese" economy characterised by commercial capital. This neat stratification is at once too simple and too sweeping.[1] For instance, in Sarawak there are clear economic differences between the so-called "Shan-Pa" and the bazaars. "Shan-Pa" signifies the rural areas where the rubber holdings are situated; the bazaars are the market centres where exchange takes place. It is true that in the First Division this difference in place and in economic background corresponds with a difference in the dialect of the inhabitants - the rural people being almost exclusively Hakka speaking, the bazaar people of other dialect groups - but the difference is not a racial one - both Hakkas and non-Hakkas are Chinese. Of course there are Malays and Dayaks in the First Division too, and they do predominate in the rubber districts and hold only a minor position in the bazaars, nevertheless 43% of the rubber planters in the First Division are Chinese. In the Third Division, moreover, there is not even a dialect difference to mark off the rural Chinese from the bazaar Chinese,for there Foochow people are found in both town and country. Thus, instead of a single economic group which may be labelled "Chinese", we find at least two groups:on the one hand, the urban Chinese, merchants and middlemen, on the other,the rural Chinese, rubber planters and primary producers.

A demographic analysis makes the situation clear in detail. In the First Division there are 21,699 Chinese[2] living in the municipality of Kuching(the capital of Sarawak), while another 40,422 live in the rural areas,[3]which, except for 11 small bazaar centres, are entirely under rubber gardens. Even among the 21,699 living in the municipality, not more than half live in the real bazaar area, for the major part of the area designated "municipal" (all, that is, but 19 streets) is also under gardens, and should thus be considered, from the economic if not the administrative point of view, as "rural".[4]

Now the Hakka people were largely farmers at home in China. In Sarawak their economic role is the same. Nearly all the labour in the rubber gardens of the First Division is provided by Hakka people. The Census Report (1947) shows that out of 62,121 Chinese in the First Division, 35,470 are Hakka, amounting to nearly one half of the total. Of this Hakka total of 35,470 only 5,730 (16%) live in the "municipal" area of Kuching. A more detailed discussion of these figures appears in a later chapter, but here it must be emphasised that they do indicate a very significant economic cleavage within the Chinese population as a whole.

The differences between the economic roles of different groups of overseas Chinese may also be seen from a consideration of the occupational distribution. The Chinese in the First Division are mainly engaged in commerce and agricultural work. As the Census Report shows, the total number of persons engaging in commerce in 1947 was 4,201 of whom 3,430 were Chinese.At the same time there were as many as 13,430 Chinese in agriculture, mainly rubber gardening. In the First Division there were altogether 8,306 people engaged in rubber production; 3,610 of these (43%) were Chinese.

These figures give some indication of the importance of avoiding overhasty generalisation about the economic status of the Chinese overseas. It is not suggested that the rural and urban economies are independent of each other; on the contrary a close and indispensable relation exists between them; one

1. The original hypothesis of "plural society" was developed by J.S.Furnivall: Netherlands India, a study of Plural Economy. (Cambridge). 1939. Furnivall himself is careful not to oversimplify his categories, which are clearly justified in his text; nevertheless it seems fairly evident that the categories he uses have been oversimplified by others, and to that extent his work has been misleading.
2. The term "Chinese" is used here, and throughout, to indicate the oversea Chinese as a racial and cultural group. No reference to questions of nationality is intended.
3. Census Report (1947).
4. Report of a Survey of Overcrowding in Kuching. (1949). Typescript.

cannot discuss one without mentioning the other. Because they concentrate upon growing an export crop the rural people depend upon the bazaars for their daily food: because they live by selling rubber the bazaar people depend upon the rural areas for their livelihood. Complementary differences are none the less differences, however, and the economic role of the rubber farmer, working the land, providing the labour, is essentially different from that of the shopkeeper, collecting and handing on the primary product and distributing provisions and credit.

The merchant class can be further subdivided into (a) the small bazaar-shopkeepers who supply daily provisions to the farmers and act as middlemen in the rubber trade and (b) the big exporting firms in Kuching and Sibu. It is only the comparatively backward nature of the economy of Sarawak which masks the fact that many Chinese may also be found in the "topmost" (or "European") economic stratum.[1]

Now if we are to tackle the sociological problems of the overseas Chinese communities it is essential to emphasise the economic cleavages within them. It is true, for instance, that commerce in Sarawak is almost entirely in Chinese hands. "The Chinese" are therefore frequently blamed for the hardships suffered by the indigenous people. Yet as the above figures show the Chinese in Sarawak are far from being all moneylenders and shopkeepers. Once the significance of actual economic roles is stressed it is immediately patent that the economic position of the Chinese in the rural areas is almost identical with that of the Malays and Dayaks. In this perspective the "problem of the Chinese community" is not a separate problem at all, but a part of the general problem of the future development of the agricultural economy of Sarawak as a whole. Moreover, once the economic structure of the country as a whole is considered, it is comparatively easy to understand the emergence of this strong Chinese commercial element. Similar economic situations in other parts of the world demand the existence of a similar class, which plays an important, even indispensible, part in the maintenance of a non-industrial economy at a certain stage. One might mention the Syrians in West Africa as examples, but the situation can also exist without the marked "social visibility" which differences in race or culture give it, for example the Compradores in China, the large scale Indian merchants in India, and similar developments among people of European descent in the early days in America or Australia.

Thus for purposes of analysis it is imperative to divide the total community of overseas Chinese in Sarawak, according to differences of economic role, into rural and bazaar communities. But this division has more than a purely economic significance, for the differences in economic role are accompanied by differences in social structure. The distinction between rural and urban Chinese in Sarawak finds no expression in such things as different dress or speech or manners or education - as do class distinctions in England, for example; in fact, to the casual eye there are only the differences in location, in dialect (in the First Division) and, to some extent, in standards of living. Beneath these, however, are important sociological differences: in the rural areas socio-economic relations are based mainly upon clanship, in the bazaars occupational groupings, which, as we have seen, often include clan relationships but also stretch far beyond them, take pride of place.

Thus if we are to study the operations of clanship and occupational grouping in the overseas Chinese community, it is simplest to study the one in the economic environment of the rural areas, and the other in the setting of the bazaars. This is the task of the next four chapters.

V

C L A N S H I P

Shortly after my arrival in Sarawak I had occasion to visit a certain Mr T'ien (田) who lived at some distance from Kuching. I took with me a young

1. As in Singapore and the Netherlands Indies. See Furnivall op. cit., p.410.

student friend named Yang (楊). On our arrival we were treated with all the ordinary marks of hospitality, but there was perhaps a hint of constrained politeness in the air until our host, on enquiring, was told that my friend's surname was also T'ien. Immediately all constraint was dropped, and we were both treated as members of the family. I later asked my friend why he had lied about his surname. He told me that he had learned the value of the "surname bond" when travelling in Dutch Borneo, where he had never failed to find help from other Yangs once he had made his own name known. Later, I myself experienced the advantages of the intricate network of this kind of surname relationship. I could always find hospitality with other T'iens anywhere in the Colony, and in each district I would be told of T'iens whom I would meet at my next stopping place. Conversely, any T'ien coming to Kuching from the rural districts, no matter how far distant, would be likely to call upon me, his "Doctor Kinsman".

The fiction is, of course, that all who share the same surname must be patrilineally related, however remote the degree of kinship. This bond thus unites all who use the same Chinese character for their surname, no matter from what part of China they come or what dialect they speak.[1] In China the surname was until recently strictly exogamous, and remains so to a very marked degree, especially in rural districts and in the North. Members of the same surname group may address and refer to each other as "clan brothers".

This surname group as a whole may be described as the widest Chinese clan group.[2] The term clanship usually[3] refers to a relationship based upon presumed but not actually traceable common unilineal descent. It may be argued that for the Chinese situation this definition is inappropriate, since it is well known that long written genealogies exist in which descent is recorded and carefully traced step by step, often back to the Chou dynasty (1060-256) B.C.) or even earlier.[4] Only the well-to-do, however, have been able to keep such written genealogies, or to read them. Although the ambition to possess a genealogy book is almost universal, yet for the very large majority of Chinese detailed tracing of distant relationships is impossible. In any case no really complete record of any single surname group in China exists.[5]

The whole surname group, or clan, is variously referred to in Chinese. Perhaps tsu (族) is the most commonly used term, but like the others it has no single, precise referent. The widest clan is the whole surname group.

---

1. Difference of dialect may involve quite marked difference in pronunciation of the surname: this makes no difficulty if the Chinese character is the same. For example the character 田 is pronounced T'ien in Mandarin, but Ch'ann in Fukienese (Hokkien). Both pronunciations are found in Sarawak, and users of both consider each other mutually related.

2. The Chinese language has several terms, most of which are usually translated "clan". The most common, tsu and fang, are referred to in the text.

3. Following the normal usage of British anthropologists.

4. The historical accuracy or otherwise of traced genealogies is irrelevant to the definition. See Evans-Pritchard: The Nuer. Oxford (1940).

5. On the other hand even the least literate peasant usually knows to which generation in the supposed clan genealogy he belongs. Generation order is preserved in naming. The first character of a child's name being the same for all members of the same generation.
   The custom of keeping written genealogies in China had its origin in the Chou dynasty (c.1050 - 256 B.C.), but actually became popular in Han times (206 B.C. - 219 A.D.). The Golden Age of genealogy keeping was in the "Northern and Southern dynasties" (420 A.D. - 581 A.D.), during which period the government ran a special office of genealogical records. From the T'ang dynasty (618 A.D. - 906 A.D.) the study of genealogies declined, but the Chinese National Library in Peking to-day has a special department for genealogies and a very large collection. The editing of genealogies has a defined method and order, with certain fixed rules, for sub-division and so forth. For a full account see: Yang Tien-Hsui "Introduction to the Study of Chinese Genealogies" Quarterly Bulletin of Chinese Bibliography. Vol.3, Nos.1-2, 1941, pp.9-35, Vol.6, Nos.3-4, 1945, pp.17-39, (In Chinese).

This includes all male descendants of clan members. Daughters are regarded as belonging to their fathers' clan; but women's clan membership is not considered of the same quality as men's - women take no part in clan ceremonies, for example.[1] Like most wide groups based upon the recognition of unilineal descent the Chinese surname group is subject to segmentation. Bearers of the same surname may be scattered throughout China. The widest clan therefore cannot be a corporate group with an organised structure. In China, then, agnatic descent groups of a corporate nature are usually localised segments of the surname groups, often occupying a single village or group of villages.[2] These localised sub-clans, as I shall call them here, are also termed tsu in Chinese. the localised sub-clan is usually organised under the leadership of a recognised head, whose jural authority over all members might in the past be absolute, and is often still very strong. The localised sub-clan usually possesses clan lands, on which the ancestral tomb, symbol of local clan solidarity, is found, and from which the proceeds go to maintain the local clan's ancestral hall. This ancestral hall was in the past, and in many cases still remains, the centre for the education of clan members and for the organisation of mutual help amongst them.

The localised sub-clans necessarily vary considerably in size and generation depth. They are not undifferentiated groups, but usually comprise several genealogically related segments, frequently termed fang (房 , literally 'room' or 'house'). Members of a group fang can always trace their common descent and the fang group might therefore be termed a lineage.

Thus, speaking very broadly indeed, and recognising the existence of almost infinite variety in custom, we may say that the widest clan, or surname group, comprises a very large number of dispersed localised sub-clans, whose members may or may not be able to trace their mutual kinship, and which are probably sub-divided into lineages. In one village in Chao An (Fukien province), for example, the localised sub-clan contains four such villages, each comprising a number of sub-lineages.[3] Each lineage is considered responsible for a certain proportion (usually an equal proportion) of the upkeep of the local clan's ancestral hall.

From this particular village, T'ien Chu,[4] a large number of immigrants has come to Sarawak. It can therefore provide an illustration of the ways in which the clan system of China has been transplanted overseas. About 50 years ago, a certain T'ien K'ou, a member of the fourth lineage was reported to have made a fortune in Sarawak. Partly at his invitation and partly because they thought it a promising move emigrants from T'ien Ch'u came to join him. A portion of the localised sub-clan was thus transported almost wholesale to

1. A woman's connexion with her husband's clan is symbolised at the wedding ceremony by her formal kow-tow to his ancestral tablets and tombs, and was perpetuated in the old days by the absolute ban upon widow re-marriage. (A form of matrilocal marriage also exists in China whereby a sonless man may 'adopt' his son-in-law, who then takes his father-in-law's name and becomes a full member of his clan).

2. The full localisation of agnatic descent groups, producing the wellknown 'clan villages' is not equally developed in different parts of China. It is perhaps noteworthy for the present study that this localisation is said to be most pronounced in the Yangtze valley and in the provinces of Fukien and Kwangtung, from which the majority of emigrants come. Marion J. Levy jr:The Family Revolution in Modern China, (Harvard U.P.) 1949, p.50; also Hsien Chin Hu: The Common Descent Group in China and its Functions, Viking Fund Publication in Anthropology, No.10. (New York) 1948.

3. I am not here concerned with the family organisation (chia 家) which has had much more adequate treatment in the published (English) material, notably by Fei Hsiao-Tung, Olga Lang, M. Levy. The chia comprises an agnatic core, with affinal relatives. The core of the chia is, of course, a sub-lineage. In the peasant families this is usually only 2 generations deep, or less; among the gentry it may be much bigger.

4. Note that in this Fukien village the clan name is given to the village as to the village as a whole. No other surnames can be found there.

Sarawak, and their descendants to-day are intensely conscious of their common origin. Together they form the Chao An branch of the T'ien clan in Sarawak.[1]

The actual division of the localised sub-clan is interesting. From the first and second lineages in Chao An there were no emigrants. The third lineage now has between five and six hundred and the fourth lineage rather more than one hundred descendants living in Kuching. Four fourth lineage households remain in Chao An, but the number of third lineage members still there, if any, is not known in Sarawak.

The differences between these two groups of T'iens descendants of the third and fourth lineages respectively, are quite marked. The latter is the smaller group, and the richer. The thirteen households of this group are in the residential area of Kuching, their heads are all engaged in commerce. The household groups are fairly large. Descendants of the third lineage are more numerous, their occupations mainly in unskilled labour, and their 107 household groups, comprising simple families only, are nearly all to be found in one particular area, Sekarna, on the outskirts of Kuching. Sekarna is inhabited by other Chao An people, but the T'iens predominate. Of the 175 pupils on the register of the Fifth Chung Hwa School in Sekarna, 145 are of Chao An origin and 63 of these are T'iens. This pattern of clan concentration can also be illustrated from the figures of employment. Before the Japanese war there were four groups of wharf labourers in Kuching. The head of each group was called T'ien. Each kept a shop-house in which he lived together with the other members of his wharf-labourers,"company" (Kongsi) - all of them kinsmen. Proceeds from the wharf labour were pooled by each company, money for rent and food was subtracted and the remainder divided into equal shares of which the head received two and the others one each. Since the war this exclusive T'ien control of wharf labour has broken down; there are now nine other,new, wharf labour gangs and only 54 of the total 330 wharf labourers are called T'ien.[2] But this clan still predominates among those from Chao An, accounting for 43·3% of the total membership of the Chao An Association.[3]

Between the two groups of Chao An T'iens, descendants of the third and fourth T'ien Chu lineages, there exist bonds of clan solidarity, though enthusiasm for clan affairs comes mainly from the poorer branch, as might be expected. The richer group, however, have produced the more strictly formal organisation - at least on paper - for their members provide one of the only four examples in Sarawak of a formally listed clan Association.[4] This Association was included in the Government list in 1946, under the name Chan Chinn Ann, which was the name of the business run by the original T'ien settler, T'ien K'ou. The initiative for the formation of a listed Association came from the present chairman who is commonly regarded as the head of all the Sarawak T'iens. This man is a descendant of the original T'ien K'ou, but owes his dominance less to descent than to his personal abilities. The main task of Chinese clanship in Sarawak, combination for mutual help,is organised much more informally.

The economic significance of this informal type of clan structure is discussed in detail in the next chapter. It finds interesting ritual expression

---

1. The second branch comprise the Hakka speaking T'iens from Hweilai. See below.

2. The Chairman of the Wharf Labourers' Trade Union (1949) is a T'ien (Ch'an).

3. T'iens in Sekarna are also pigbreeders and, a few of them, carpenters and masons. The women, if employed, tend to follow the usual Chao An tradition as maidservants.

4. The others are the Hsu Association, and the T'ang and Wong Associations in Sibu. There is also a Shen Association, which is simply a branch of an Association of the same clan in Singapore. This last is a very large organisation, drawing members from six Chinese provinces (Kansu, Chekiang, Anwhei, Kwangtung, Kwangli, Fukien) and having branches in Kuching, Malacca, Bangkok, Bajuaga and several other towns in the Nan Yang. Clan Associations in Singapore listed as such in the (Chinese) Directory of Chinese Schools and Associations (1948) number 109.

at times of "crises de passage", such as weddings and funerals at which the attendance of representatives of all sub-lineages must be invited, and in the annual ceremony of "sweeping the ancestral tomb" at the Ch'ing-Ming festival[1] It is noteworthy that at this annual festival the most active participants are those from the third lineage - the poorer group of Chao An T'iens.

The Chao An T'iens are, however, only one of the T'ien groups in Sarawak. There is also a Hakka speaking group from Hweilai (Kwangtung). Of these there are about 3,000 individuals occupying some 475 households of a local clan in China, and 697 individuals in 281 households in Sarawak. The history of the arrival of these people in Sarawak has not been recorded, but it was probably fairly recent, since a very large number of them can still describe the plan of the local clan village at home, and the distribution of lineage groups in it, in considerable detail. One member of this Hweilai T'ien group owns a genealogy book which he had copied from that of his sub-lineage in China. It deals only with that sub-lineage, however, and is therefore incomplete.[2]

The Hweilai T'iens in Sarawak are found in 17 different villages scattered almost throughout the First Division, but clustering mainly at the 15th and 22nd mile points along the Simanggang Road. A few have recently moved into the Second and Third Divisions, but formerly nearly all the members of this group were to be found in and around Seniawen. Apart from about a score of small shopkeepers all are peasant farmers. Their organisations as a group is informal, but none the less real, and as usual its main function is to provide mutual help. The leaders of the group are a couple of T'iens, one in Bata Kuwa and one in Seniawen, who as the richest members, and therefore the largest grantors of credit, have a commanding position.

We can see, therefore, how the local clan of China suffers a sea-change on the voyage to Sarawak. The Chao An T'iens and the Hweilai T'iens each regard themselves as a single group, but these groups are not strictly localised, their formal organisation is very flexible, and their function is mainly economic. At the same time neither group is as clearly distinct as a local clan in China. On the contrary, each is much more realistically considered simply as a segment of the T'ien group in Sarawak as a whole. Between the Chao An and Hweilai T'iens no genealogical relationship is traced, and certainly the two groups are not territorially contiguous. On the other hand, their sense of mutual solidarity may be said to be considerably greater than that existing between two separate local clans of the same surname group in China. At the time of writing no members of the Hweilai group have joined the T'ien Association, but, as we have seen, Associations based upon clanship are very infrequent in Sarawak, and the T'ien Association does not even include all the Chao An T'iens. A sense of "belonging together" undoubtedly exists between Chao An and Hweilai T'iens. Mutual economic assistance is given by and to members of both groups without apparent distinction.

Mutual T'ien solidarity even finds ritual expression. At the Ch'ing Ming festival, for example, it is always a joint Chao An and Hweilai party that performs the ceremony of sweeping the ancestral tombs. It appears that this linkage was first made several years ago at the instigation of the Hweilai group who desired to cash in on their connexion with the rich and influential T'iens (of the fourth Chao An lineage) in Kuching. As the two groups do not possess a common ancestor (and even if such a one had existed he would not have died in Sarawak), there cannot possibly be a common ancestral tomb. The difficulty was not insurmountable. In 1925 a special mock tomb - containing, of course, no corpse - was constructed in the Chao An cemetery. This monument was carefully inscribed with a reference to the origin of the T'ien surname group in China, and an expression of hope for continued prosperity "by all the descendants who worshipped here together and erected this tomb in the 7th lunar

1. 106 days after the Winter solstice, usually early in the 3rd moon of the Lunar Calendar. A second rite at the ancestral tomb is performed at the Mid Autumn festival.

2. It is also historically quite valueless, having actually been compiled from several sources. The order of generations, however, seems to be accurate. This is ascertainable from the method of naming already mentioned (ftnt: 5 p. 22). The generation names are fixed in advance, and can usually be recited with the rhythm and rhyme of verse.

month of the year 1923".[1]

In most Hakka clans clan solidarity finds expression also in the development of certain clan secrets. These are all concerned with peculiar forms of pugilism. T'ien clan members in Sarawak tell the story of a certain T'ien ancestor, a fisherman, who suffered repeated insult and injury from his Teochow neighbours. Finally, able to bear it no longer, he put himself in the hands of a famous Shansi blacksmith, a master in the art of self-defence. Under this man's training fisherman T'ien rapidly became an expert, and returned home with certain secret techniques which made him invincible. The skills which he handed on to his clan brothers remain the secret of the T'ien clan to this day, and, although they are no longer learnt by all T'ien boys as a matter of course, they are still very highly valued,[2] and form a kind of secret emblem of clan membership.[3]

A second external mark of the mutual solidarity of the two sections of the T'ien surname group in Sarawak is the habit by which members of both address each other in kinship terms. This goes beyond the mere attribution of clan brotherhood which was referred to in the description of surname groups in China. Within each section there are, of course, still known genealogical links, which even if not fully traced back make it possible for every individual to know at the very least to which generation he belongs. All Chao An T'iens and all Hweilai T'iens know the order of generations within their own groups, and are thus able to refer to those of the next senior generation as "uncles" and "aunts", and those in the next junior generation as "nephews" and "nieces" and so forth.[4] Chao An T'iens address Hweilai T'iens similarly, difference of dialect notwithstanding, but as actual relationships are untraceable questions of seniority are settled entirely by considerations of age and social prestige.

This ascription of definite generation status to all T'iens in Sarawak is also extended to cover two other individuals with the same surname who are by origin attached neither to the Chao An nor the Hweilai group. One of these is a trader from Foochow, who despite his place of origin is a member of the Chao An dialect association; the other was myself. I found myself drawn into nearly all clan activities, and was made the recipient of clan help which I was expected to offer to others in my turn. I also took part in the Ch'ing Ming festival in 1949. My exact position in the local T'ien generation order was a frequent topic of enquiry. It proved impossible to explain that a T'ien from Kunming probably had no genealogical connexion at all with T'iens from Chao An and Hweilai.

The total membership of the T'ien surname group in Sarawak in 1949 may be summarised thus:

---

1. In China the ancestral tomb is usually situated on the ancestral lands held by the local clan, in Sarawak there is no clan land, and the T'ien monument is therefore placed in the cemetery used by the most influential T'ien segment.

2. Informants mentioned in confidence that there existed at the present time five T'ien people in the Nan Yang who had a complete mastery of the boxing skills.

3. It is told how in the old days the T'ien boxing technique proved its value in inter-clan strife. A T'ien girl married unhappily into another clan, for instance, could get help from her clansmen by sending a traditional message. The wording of this message provides another example of a clan secret, for the girl would say: "Have you a hall big enough to put all the umbrellas in?", the reference being to the alleged T'ien custom of always carrying an umbrella under the left arm.

4. The Chao An T'iens know their generation order by number only, tracing 20 generations. The Hweilai group trace between 15 and 19 generations, and can give not only the numerical order but also the generation name (i.e. the Chinese character used for the first word of the personal name of each individual of a single generation). Clan generation names were strictly used by the Hweilai T'iens until recently. Nowadays parents tend to name their children according to their own personal whim, but the "correct" generation name, though not used, is still known and will be given on enquiry.

T A B L E   4

T'IEN   CLAN   IN   SARAWAK   1949

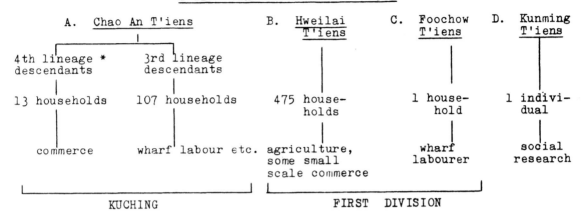

A. Chao An T'iens		B. Hweilai T'iens	C. Foochow T'iens	D. Kunming T'iens
4th lineage * descendants	3rd lineage descendants			
13 households	107 households	475 households	1 household	1 individual
commerce	wharf labour etc.	agriculture, some small scale commerce	wharf labourer	social research
KUCHING		FIRST DIVISION		

* group includes local clan leader.

    The widest group I intend to call the T'ien clan (or surname group) in
Sarawak. The Chao An and Hweilai segments I describe respectively as Chao An
and Hweilai sub-clans.[1] Within the sub-clans the term lineage can be applied
to segments of agnatic kin who actually trace their common descent.

    Leadership in the sub-clans has already been mentioned. It is not a mat-
ter of seniority, or of automatic appointment. Instead it appears to be   a
somewhat informal recognition of the pre-eminent position of a certain individual or individuals, an account of their personal qualities, and, in particular, their high economic status. The whole question of leadership among the
Chinese in Sarawak forms the subject matter of Chapter IX, but here it is
necessary to point to the marked contrast between clan leadership in Sarawak
and local clan headship in China. The most influential member of the whole
T'ien clan in Sarawak is the man whose position as founder and chairman of the
registered T'ien Association has already been described. He is thus generally regarded as the clan leader.

    It is not at all easy to state exactly what powers this informal   clan
leadership can exercise over clan members. As we shall see, the major significance of clan membership is economic, and the position of clan leader   is
chiefly important in matters concerned with immigration, but in   the jural
sphere there is at least a very strong moral compulsion to keep intra-clan disputes within the clan. For one member to sue another in Court without first
trying to settle the dispute with the help of the clan leader, or at least
gaining his approval, would be considered a grave breach of clan discipline.
A recent example illustrates this convention: One of the Hweilai members of
the T'ien clan (let us call him "A") living at Bata Kawa had a personal quarrel with a local teacher, not a T'ien. The teacher managed to get a   second
member of the T'ien clan to put up a kind of broad sheet to insult A. Before
seeking redress through the Secretary for Chinese Affairs, A first went to the
Chairman of the T'ien Association in order to inform him of the matter and get
his permission to take it to Court. A himself is quite convinced   that the
local teacher deliberately made a point of getting his T'ien friend to publish
the insulting material rather than doing it himself, with the object of put-
ting him, A, in an awkward dilemma. Had the insult been offered by a non-clan
member, A could have found some direct way of taking his revenge.

---

1. Not lineages, as common descent is not fully traced by all members.

To a considerable extent, therefore, the surname group as a whole in Sarawak takes the place of the local clan in China. Regardless of separate local origin in China, and regardless of "scatter" in Sarawak, all the T'iens there regard themselves as a single group, behaving much as a local clan behaves in China, and even joining together in the supreme ritual demonstration of local clanship - the annual sweeping of the ancestral tomb. On the other hand the clan in Sarawak is not a landholding group, it maintains no ancestral hall or clan education system, its jural competence is limited and its organisation and leadership essentially informal.

What has been said here of the T'ien clan applies in general terms to almost all the other surname groups in Sarawak. We have already seen[1] that dominance in the Hakka speaking group belongs to immigrants from the Hoppu division of the Kityang Hsien in Kwangtung. It appears that in this division there are 17 surname groups, 13 of them large. Their names, and the estimated size of their membership may be seen from Table 5. From 10 of them large numbers of emigrants have come to Sarawak, where they may be found widely distributed throughout the First Division.

T A B L E   5

NAMES AND NUMBER OF MEMBERS OF HOPPU CLANS

Names in		Estimated number of Members in China[2]
Mandarin	Hakka	
Chang*	Chong	28,000
Liu**	Liu	17,000
Ts'ai**	Chhoa	15,000
Wang**	Wong	10,000
Li**	Li	10,000
Yang*	Yong	6,500
Wen*	Wun	4,000
Tang*	T'en	2,500
Pei*	P'ui	2,000
Han	Hon	1,500
Chin	Hiu	1,500
Chen	Chin	1,500
Wu	Ng	500
Others		1,000
	Total:	101,000

Note: Those clans which have wide ramifications in Sarawak are marked with one asterisk; the most widely spread with two.

The most largely represented of these Hoppu clans in Sarawak has the surname Ts'ai. This clan, as we have seen, may be called the dominant clan of

---

1. Table 3, p. 16 and Table 4, p.18.

2. As estimated by clan members.

the dominant group of the Hakka Association.[1] Its structure may be described as both more close and more informal than that of the T'ien clan.   All the Ts'ai in Sarawak are members of the same (Hakka) dialect group, and even came from the same district (Hoppu). It is true that in China many would belong to distinct local clans, but there would appear to be a much closer relationship in genealogical terms between different members of the Ts'ai clan in Sarawak, and, say, a T'ien from Hweilai and a T'ien from Chao An.   On the other hand, the Ts'ai clan in Sarawak observes no joint Ch'ing Ming ceremony, shares no special pugilistic secrets, boasts no registered clan Association. All Ts'ai address each other by the correct terms of kinship in generation order, however, and the present most influential Ts'ai holds a genealogy book   which traces his own lineage to its connexion with the senior local clan in Hoppu.[1] This man, again a wealthy trader, is regarded as the leader of the Ts'ai clan in Sarawak.

The very large majority of the Ts'ai are peasants, however. **They are** concentrated mainly between the 24th and 32nd mile on the Semanggang   road, where in some places they form more than 50% of the Chinese population.

In contrast both with the T'ien clan which includes members of different dialect groups, and with Ts'ai who all originate from the same division of the same hsien in China, is the Yang clan. All the members of this surname group in Sarawak are Hakka speaking, but they are drawn from four different, though neighbouring, districts in Kwangtung: Hoppu, Hweilai, Tap'u and Mei.   There is no registered clan association, and no joint celebration of the Ch'ing Ming festival, but kinship terms are used and the correct generation   characters known.[2] The Yangs, like the T'iens have their own secret methods of fighting, which are known at least to all the rural Yangs in Sarawak. A descendant of the first settler, who is said to have arrived in Miri as a trader about   70 years ago, is the present leader of the Yang clan. His position is probably buttressed by this descent, but it depends primarily upon his wealth and influence. He was at one time Chairman of the Hakka Association,   and   still plays an important part in its affairs.

About 70 members of the Yang clan are to be found scattered in Kuching, and throughout the Colony. As Table 6 shows there is no particular concentration of Yangs in Sarawak.

A consideration of the details by which other clans in Sarawak may vary from or approximate to the models of the three described here would be tedious. Enough has been said to show the broad generalities of Chinese clan organisation in Sarawak, but a word should be added concerning inter-clan   relationships. In Chapter III we have already mentioned the close   inter-connexions which have arisen over the years through the natural development of affinal links between members of different clans. Each clan is exogamous, and every individual therefore has matrilateral relatives in one other clan, and, possibly, affinal relatives in several more. These ties are ties of person to person rather than ties of individual to group, but they nevertheless form breaches, as it were, in the clan walls and create a complex network of kin relationships which helps to bind the largely endogamous Chinese group as a whole ever more firmly together. It is worth pointing out here, too, that the basic social unit is, of course, not a unilineal group but a family. It is not part of the purpose of this study to describe overseas Chinese family organisation,

---

1. The Ts'ai surname group as a whole is believed to have had its origin in the Chiyan-Yang district in Fukien. The first 19 generations dwelt there. After a migration to the South in about 1480 A.D. (Ch'enghua period) certain members of the clan settled in Hoppu where a fresh start was made in counting the generations. In Sarawak to-day members of the 17th - 21st generations of this second clan era are to be found.

2. The character for the 18th Yang generation (the generation of the first settlers) is pronounced Fang, the 19th Chang,   the 20th Hwang, and the 21st Ch'ang. The first three have been constantly used in naming. It is significant of a change in social custom that the last is not so used;   present day parents choose names from their personal preference instead; the correct generation character can always be elicited on enquiry. Cf. p.26 note.

but it is relevant, if somewhat obvious, to note here that the family contains
members of more than one clan.

Inter-clan relationships are further affected by a variety of traditional clan alliances. Sometimes the members of two or more surname groups may
consider themselves clan brothers together, rationalising the situation by reference to certain traditional tales. For example, it is said that once   in
Chinese history four individuals named Liu, Kwang, Chang and Chou became"sworn
brothers", and therefore people with these four surnames to-day consider themselves kin.[1] Clan alliances are common in South China. They follow no fixed
rules and their membership varies from place to place.[2]

As we shall see in the following chapters, clan relationships have a different significance for the relatively richer, urban and the poorer, largely
rural Chinese in Sarawak. We have already hinted at this difference when we
described the membership of the registered T'ien Association and   suggested
that for the rich and influential members of the Association was a source of
prestige, while for the rest, excluded from registered membership,   general
clan solidarity was far more important for personal, economic reasons.   This
difference is illustrated at the T'iens' Ch'ing Ming ceremonial, which,   as a
general rule, is performed exclusively by members of the poorer class.

The greater significance of clanship in the rural districts and for the
poorer people is further illustrated by the figures of clan distribution.Mem-
bers of the merchant class are scattered, or live independently in Kuching or
Sibu; members of the peasant and labouring class tend to congregate in clan
groups in the poorer suburbs and in the countryside. The following tables show
the distribution of clans among the rural Chinese in the First Division.

T A B L E   6

CLAN RELATIONSHIPS OF OVERSEAS CHINESE LIVING ALONG THE SIMANGGANG
ROAD ~ ALL HAKKA.

Place	Total no. of students*	No. & % of Hakka students	Place of Origin of Majority of Hakka students and No. & % of this majority to the total no. of students in each (Sarawak) area.	No. of Hakka students from the dominant clan (Names pronounced in Mandarin)
			**	
4½ mile	172	92(56%)	Hweichow 38 (22%) Hoppu 18 (9%) Hweilai 15 (8.7%)	Chen 24 Wang 15 Wu 10 Yang 12 Lo 8 Lai 8 Chang 9 others 86
7½ "	132	122(93%)	Hweichow 34 (26%) Hoppu 46 (34%) Hweilai 26 (20%)	Chen 21 Wen 15 Cheng 14 Ts'ai 12 Tseng 10 Lai 8 Others 50
10 "	122	133(92·5%)	Hweichow 47 (37%) Hoppu 69 (56%) Hweilai 12 (9%)	Wang 27 Yang 15 Hao 12 Ts'ai 11 Lai 9 Chen 9 Li 8

* & ** on following page.

1. In Singapore there is a registered Association, Gu Cheng Huay Goan by name,
   which draws its members from these four groups.
2. In Henghua, for instance, the T'ien clan is allied with the Cheng, Hu, Yen
   and Yee; among the Hakka people, on the other hand, T'ien (Chan) is allied
   with Yao and Yee. Clan alliances are most conspicuous in cases of   inter-
   clan feud.

TABLE 6 - cont.

15 Mile	50	43(86%)	Hweilai	25(50%)	Others 31 Cheng 11 Chen 9 Lai 8	
			Hoppu	7(14%)	Li 7 Others 15	
17 "	169	148(86%)	Hweilai	83(49%)	P'eng 26 T'ien 23	
			Hoppu	45(25%)	Lai 21 Wen 16 Li 15	
			Lufeng	20(11%)	Yang 15 Others 53	
20 "	83	70(84·3%)	Hoppu	31(37%)	Chen 13 Wang 12 Wen 9	
			Hweilai	21(21%)	Lin 7 Ts'ai 5 Li 5	
			Lufeng	12(14%)	Others 32	
24 "	189	181(95%)	Hoppu	148(80%)	Liu 29 Ts'ai 23 Cheng 22 Chen 21 T'ien 16 Wang 14 Yang 11 Li 10 Others 43	
29 "	75	73(97%)	Hoppu	52(69%)	Ts'ai 15 Liu 13 Li 12 Chen 10 Pei 7 Others 23	
32 "	150	148(99%)	Hoppu	109(72%)	Ts'ai 72 Yang 19 Wang 18 Liu 16 Li 13 Others 15	
35 "	121	121(100%)	Hoppu	104(84%)	Ts'ai 62 Liu 17 Li 17 Chung 11 Wang 7 Others 7	
Serian	142	119(81%)	Hoppu	74(50%)	Wang 22 Yang 21	
			Kaying	30(21%)	Ts'ai 19 Liu 13	
			Tappu	15(10%)	Chang 18 Others 59	
Teba-kang	58	58(100%)	Kaying	23(40%)	Chu 25 Chung 10	
			Tappu	15(25%)	Wang 10 Others 13	

* This information was collected by consulting the registers kept
in the various Chung Hwa Schools. The well-known eagerness for
education among all classes of overseas Chinese, even the poor-
est, ensures that the School registers give a fairly representative picture of the general situation.

** An area covering Tungkun, Paoan and Hweiyang Hsien. In Sarawak
the Hweichow people are largely concentrated around the bazaar
area of Kuching where they work as market-gardeners.

The Table refers to the Chinese living along the Simanggang Road. It
shows clearly how most of the members of a large clan live near, or fairly
near, each other. In other words, although there are no clan villages, and
the localised sub-clan of South China does not exist, yet clan relationships
do tend to be localised. Amongst the poorer classes almost every clan has its
local centre, around which its wider ramifications are gathered. All the large
Hweilai clans, for example, have their "home base" at Batu Kawa, and extend
from there eastwards to the 4½ mile mark, southwards to the 20th mile and
south-east to Seniawen. They hold a predominant position over an area of about
250 square miles. This does not mean that scattered members of these clans
are not found in any other districts, but when they are so found they are always in minor, unimportant, uninfluential positions. Within their "home base"
area, however, the Hweilai clans are dominant in every aspect of social life,
their members forming more than half the total population. The "home bases"
of the large Hoppu clans are the strip of territory along the Simanggang Road

from the 20th mile to the terminus at Serian, and all the rural coastal strips in the First Division.

Map 3 translates Table 6 into visual terms. The hatched areas indicate the different districts in which the Hakka clans, grouped according to their place of origin in China, are congregated. The outlines of these areas in the diagram is not intended to show the exact location of members of these groups of clans. Instead, the diagram depicts only the "home bases" of each group, and must be read in conjuction with Table 6. It can easily be seen how the Hweichow clans are concentrated near Kuching, the Lufeng near Bau; the Hweilai spread rather further afield, while the Hoppu are to be found everywhere, though their areas of major settlement are in the South towards Serian. The appearance of a small group of Kaying clans in the areas of Serian and Tebaking seems at first sight to contradict the principle of clan localisation. But it is easily explained by the proximity of these areas to the Dutch frontier. The present study refers only to the British side, but the Kaying people spread right across into Dutch territory, where, in fact, they have their "home base". All the Kaying clans on the British side of the frontier areas ramify from this base.

The next two tables show the clan relationships in the Bau area, and in the rural districts along the coast in the First Division. These figures also have been taken from the local school registers.

T A B L E   7

CLAN RELATIONSHIP AMONG THE OVERSEAS CHINESE LIVING ALONG THE ROAD FROM KUCHING TO BAU

Place	Total no. of students	No. & % of Hakka students	Place of Origin of Majority of Hakka students and No. & % of this Majority to the total no. of students in each (Sarawak) area.		No. of Hakka students from the dominent clan (Names pronounced in Mandarin)
Batu Kawa Area					
Bazaar	147	143 (97%)	Hweilai	68 (46%)	Ts'ai 36 Wen 30
			Hoppu	58 (39%)	Chen 20 Wang 10
					Chang T'ien 7
					Others 35
Sejijak	30	24 (80%)	Hoppu	16 (50%)	Ts'ai 14 Wen 3
			Hweilai	5 (16%)	Wang 3 others 10
Tengah	24	24 (100%)	Hoppu	20 (83%)	Chang 11 Ts'ai 9
					Others 10
Tapang	38	38 (100%)	Hoppu	17 (45%)	Chang 12 Ts'ai 8
			Hweilai	9 (23%)	Wang 6 Others 12
S. Moryan	47	29 (61%)	Hoppu	17 (36%)	Wang 10 Ts'ai 6
			Hweilai	11 (23%)	Chang 4 Others 27
Ginchuseng	44	44 (100%)	Hoppu	22 (50%)	Wang 9 Ts'ai 8 Lai 8
			Hweilai	20 (46%)	Chang 7 Chen 6
					Others 6
S. Lubok	31	28 (90%)	Hweilai 23	(70%)	Lai 9 P'eng 6
					T'ien 6 Others 10

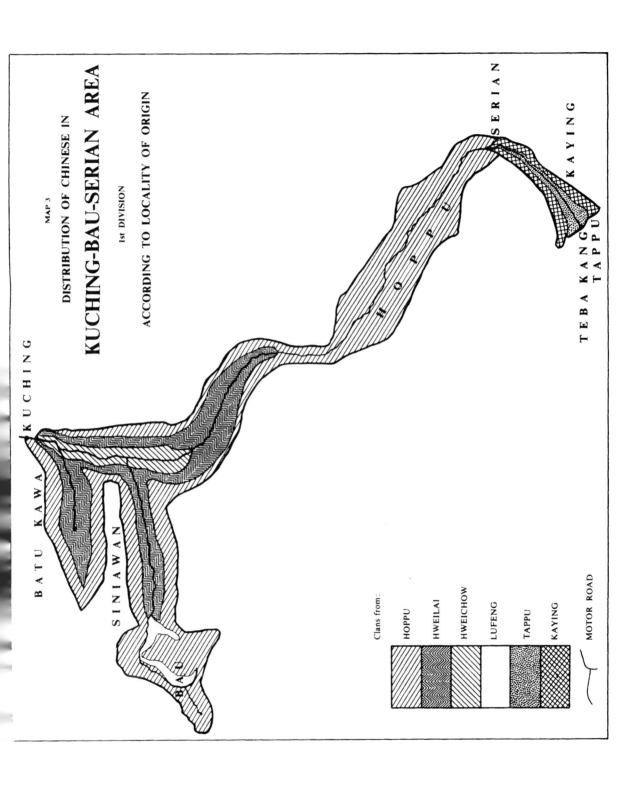

MAP 3

DISTRIBUTION OF CHINESE IN

KUCHING-BAU-SERIAN AREA

1st DIVISION

ACCORDING TO LOCALITY OF ORIGIN

KUCHING

BATU KAWA

SINIAWAN

BAU

HOPPU

SERIAN

KAYING

TEBA KANG
TAPPU

Clans from:

HOPPU

HWEILAI

HWEICHOW

LUFENG

TAPPU

KAYING

MOTOR ROAD

TABLE 7 - cont.

Siniawan	181	138 (77%)	Hoppu 68 (37%) Hweilai 38 (21%) Hai-Lu- feng 32 (17%)	Wang 35 T'ien 22 Wen 20 Li 16 Chang 12 Others 76
Buso	107	105 (98%)	Hoppu 82 (76%)	Liu 25 Ts'ai 17 Lo 13 Wen 11 Chen 11 Li 9 Others 21
Tundong	53	42 (79%)	Hoppu 23 (43%) Hai-Lu- feng 15 (28%)	Wang 11 Pei 9 Li 7 Wen 6 Ts'ai 5 Liu 4 Others 11

Bau Area

Bazaar	149	135 (91%)	Hoppu 72 (48%) Hai-Lu- feng 35 (23%)	Liu 28 Li 20 Lo 15 Ts'ai 11 Wen 6 Others 69
Taidon	36	32 (94%)	Hoppu 20 (55%) Hai-Lu- feng 8 (22%)	Ts'ai 11 Liu 9 Lee 9 Others 10
Jambusan	31	28 (90%)	Hoppu 22 (70%)	Li 10 Lai 6 Ts'ai Chang 4 Others 7
Sebuku	39	39 (100%)	Hoppu 31 (79%)	Liu 22 Yang 10 Others 7

T A B L E 7A

CLAN RELATIONSHIP AMONG THE OVERSEAS CHINESE LIVING IN THE COASTAL AREAS OF THE FIRST DIVISION

Place	Total No. of students	No. & % of Hakka students	Place of Origin of Majority of Hakka students and No. & % of this Majority to the total No.of students in each (Sarawak) area.	No. of Hakka students from the dominant clan (Names pronounced in Mandarin)
Rural Bazaar **Centres**				
Sematan	26	0		
Gedong	17	4 (24%)		
Bako	28	8 (28%)	Hoppu 7 (20%)	
Lundu	148	47 (31%)	Hoppu 30 (20%)	
Simunjan	108	41 (37%)	Hoppu 19 (17%)	
Pending	103	30 (29%)	Hoppu 18 (16%)	
S. Tapang	24	17 (70%)	Hoppu 16 (66 %)	Hsu 6 Wang 6 Chang 3 Lian 3 Others 4
Muara Tebas	28	26 (90%)	Hoppu 20 (70%)	Chang 12 Ts'ai 8 Others 8

TABLE 7A - cont.

Sungei Muda	39	36 (92%)	Hoppu 32 (82%)	Ts'ai 21 Chang 6 Tang 5 Others 8
Tambirat	54	40 (74%)	Hoppu 35 (64%)	Wang 13 Liu 10 Ts'ai 8 Others 23
Sambir	160	160 (100%)	Hoppu 118 (74%) Lufeng 29 (18%)	Ts'ai 42 Chen 29 Wang 15 Liu 11 Others 63
Nonok	230	228 (99%)	Hoppu 174 (76%) Hweilai 54 (23%)	Ts'ai 48 Liu 34 Wang 31 Chang 29 Lai 19 others 72
Semera	174	174 (100%)	Hoppu 86 (49%) Lufong 46 (27%) Hweilai 35 (20%)	Yang 32 Chen 28 Wen 25 Li 16 Fang 12 others 61
Jamukan	119	110 (92%)	Hoppu 75 (63%) Hweilai 35 (29%)	Weng 29 Chen 18 Lo 16 Yeh 12 Wang 10 Li 8 Others 24
Bliong	179	170 (94%)	Hoppu 117 (65%)	Yang 51 Chang 25 Wang 21 Ts'ai 10 Others 72
Santi	20	19 (95%)	Hoppu 13 (65%)	Wang 5 Wen 4 Tang 4 Kao 4 Others 3
Buntal	31	21 (67%)	Hoppu 13 (41%)	Chang 7 Yang 4 Lin 4 Others 15

The situation is very similar to that already described for the Simang-gang Road. At Pending, which is only 3 miles from Kuching, Hakka speaking people comprise only 29% of the total population, and the Hoppu clans only 17%. These figures underline the points made below about the economic status of the Hakka people and their relation to the Bazaar. The same point is also illus-trated by figures from all the smaller bazaar areas in the rural districts.In places like Simunjan, Lundu, Bako, Sematan and Gedong, where there are bazaars, the percentage of Hakka people drops steeply, even to nil in the last two places. In these rural bazaars the majority of the Chinese are members of other dia-lect groups, linked with a different economic status: for example, the Teo-chow people at Lundu and Bako, the Fukien people at Simunjan and the Canton-ese at Sematan.

The fifth columns in these three tables list the actual clan names to be found in the various districts mentioned.In other words, in the fifth co-lumn the groups of Hakka clans named according to their place of origin in China are broken down into their constituent surname groups. The tendency to clan concentration is there clearly demonstrated. Table 6, for example,shows the P'eng and T'ien clans dominating at the 17th mile, the Ch'en clan at the 4½ and 7½ mile, the Chu at Tebakang, the Liu at Bau, and so forth. The Ts'ai, being, as we have seen, so very numerous, dominate between the 24th and 32nd mile but scattered groups of Ts'ai are found almost everywhere; indeed, as is clearly shown in Table 8, the numbers of Ts'ai tend to vary more or less proportionately with the numbers of Hakka in any given district.

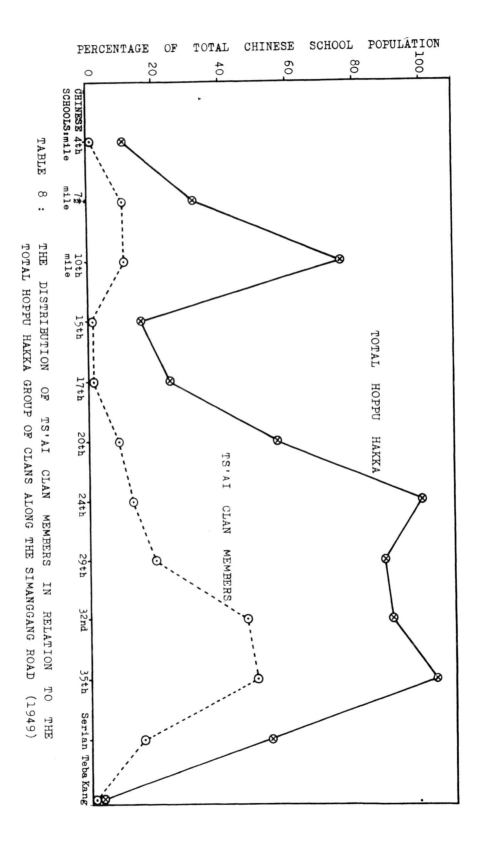

PERCENTAGE OF TOTAL CHINESE SCHOOL POPULATION

TOTAL HOPPU HAKKA

TS'AI CLAN MEMBERS

CHINESE 4th
SCHOOLS:mile   7½   10th   15th   17th   20th   24th   29th   32nd   35th   Serian Teba Kang
              mile mile

TABLE   8 :   THE   DISTRIBUTION   OF   TS'AI   CLAN   MEMBERS   IN   RELATION   TO   THE
TOTAL HOPPU HAKKA GROUP OF CLANS ALONG THE SIMANGGANG ROAD   (1949)

Nowadays it appears that the strength of clanship in the rural areas is declining. Newly opened up areas, like Nonok, Semara and Jamukan,demonstrate this clearly. Before the war, though the price of rubber was fluctuating and actually lower than it is to-day, the prices of imported goods remained at fairly reasonable and stable levels. The rural Chinese in Sarawak, on the whole, were content to work their rubber, and because new immigrants always come to join their clan relatives in the rubber districts, clan outlines remained clear. The Japanese occupation and the post-war inflation and insecurity have brought changes, however. Under the Japanese rubber was unsaleable and import was so severely limited that peasants were forced to concentrate all their energies upon the maximum growth of food crops. Since the war the future of rubber has been markedly insecure, while although its price has been higher than at any time since 1920 and in terms of money rubber growing has been more profitable than at any time since 1929, the hugely inflated prices of imported goods make its real value to the primary producer considerably less. Thus both the Japanese occupation and the post-war inflation have forced rubber-workers, small-holders and labourers alike, to find new land on which to grow some other crop.[1]

The resulting movement of population means that the dominant positions in certain localities, which certain large clans built up for themselves over a long period of time in the past, may be seriously disturbed. In Sarawak at the present time the rural Chinese are on the move. It is true that in their movements they are guided by considerations of clanship, tending to follow where other clan members have gone before, but at the same time one most important feature of clan organisation, the localised "home base", is being undermined. One example of the break-down of the old pattern is already emerging clearly in the coastal areas, where scattered among the Hoppu clans there can now be found certain Lufeng clans, which have no local connexions at all. It is possible that new patterns of clan localisation may develop in the new areas in the course of time, but this will depend upon whether or not the present structure of the rural economy remains unchanged.

VI

R U R A L   E C O N O M Y   A N D   C L A N   R E L A T I O N S H I P S

The Chinese rural economy in Sarawak hinges upon a framework of clanship. The present chapter attempts an analysis of this close interdependence of clan and economic relations. Since the rural districts of Sarawak present certain peculiar features, however, it is necessary to mention certain significant social and economic factors first.

In the First Division[2] the large majority of the population is Hakka speaking. According to the Census Report (1947) Hakka people account for 89% and 83% of the Chinese population of the Bau and Serian districts respectively. These Hakkas are mostly small rubber planters. Occasionally, after some years, a planter may manage to accumulate a certain amount of capital with which to set up as a petty merchant in a rural bazaar, but as a rule the big shops are owned by Fukienese or Teochows. This same division of labour between these dialect groups can be seen in China, where, though a few may be petty traders, the Hakkas are traditionally farmers, while in districts where Hakkas are found large scale business is usually in the hands of Teochow or

---

1. Editorial note: It must be remembered that the writer is referring to conditions in 1949.

2. Except where otherwise stated the data for this chapter are drawn entirely from the First Division. Where conditions in other areas are markedly different this fact is indicated either in the text or in footnotes.

other people in the towns.[1]

Of the economically significant factors, pride of place should probably be given to the extreme difficulty of communications, which affects both the form of business transactions and the general mode of living. In the first Division there are only two motor roads, connecting Kuching with the District Headquarters at Bau and at Serian respectively. Apart from these, and a network of single-track footpaths, all communication is by water. The local streams are shallow, usually negotiable only at high tide, and often fouled with timber. The Chinese have at least some advantage over the indigenous population in that they are largely concentrated near the sea coast or along one or other of the roads.[2]

The average density of population in the whole of Sarawak is 12 per square mile. About two thirds of the total population is concentrated in the First Division, however, where the figure for the rural areas is approximately 39 per square mile.[3] Although this figure indicates a much higher density than that for the rest of the Colony, yet the people are actually very thinly distributed. There are few aggregated groups of houses. All the Chinese planters build their dwellings in the middle of their holdings. Thus they are cut off not only from the source of foodstuffs and other daily necessities in the bazaars but also from easy contact with their neighbours. The following Table is a sampling study to show the distance of these jungle huts from the bazaar. The figures were collected by asking the students of the Chung Hwa School, at the 32nd mile on the Simmanggang Road, how long they each took to walk to school.

TABLE 9

DISTANCE FROM SCHOOL

Time taken to walk to school (Minutes)	Number of School Students
Below 15 minutes	11
15 to 30 "	17
30 " 60 "	25
60 " 90 "	9
90 " 120 "	5
Above 120 " (2 hours)	3
Total :	70

This gives a rough picture of the isolation of families in the rural districts.[4] At the same time it must not be forgotten that there are no established roads; the walk has to be made over swampy land, on which fresh rain falls almost every day. The frequent pole bridges are narrow and ricketty. Because rubber plots are all small, the daily production of rubber is also very small, and it is possible for the few sheets to be carried to the bazaar on a man's shoulders. Whenever a visit is made to buy groceries, rubber sheets are

---

1. In the Third Division planters and petty merchants are mainly Foochow speaking; larger scale business is again run by Teochows and Fukienese. From the material available it is not possible to state whether the relative status of these groups is the same as it would have been in China - where Foochow speaking people are found in commercial business as well as in agriculture.

2. See map 3 facing p.32 above.

3. Census Report (1947), pp.18, 42.

4. The ages of the students asked ranged between 12 and 18 years, the majority being about 14. School hours are from 9 - 12, and from 1 or 2 to 4 o'clock. Obviously few children can go home for a mid-day meal. Most have an inadequate snack of cold rice and water. The large majority also work on the family plots, sometimes for several hours before starting for school in the mornings.

taken in for exchange. More bulky or awkward goods, such as coconuts, atap, sugar and pigs, must travel by canoe through the ditches which drain the rubber plots, and which are only deep enough at high tide.

This difficulty of communication in the rural districts accounts for some phenomena which would otherwise seem very difficult to explain. For instance, in a small place called Bliong the main crop is coconuts. The local bazaar people trade in coconuts, but although they live in one of the big coconut producing areas of the Colony they do not always buy their coconuts locally. When the tides are low local porterage overland from plantation to bazaar costs about 80 cents per bag, but carriage from Kuching to Bliong by motor launch, at any time, costs only 50 cents a bag.[1]

It is generally recognised that agricultural work has its own peculiar nature, in that it is not equally distributed over the whole working year. As a result agricultural workers, unlike factory employees, do not draw a constant wage. All agricultural workers suffer from slack periods, though these are not necessarily the same with different crops. Several of the commercial crops in Sarawak have a long growing period. Rubber trees can only be tapped after six or seven years; coconuts come into bearing after 4 years. Neither of these crops has an annual "harvest" period, but coconuts are only gathered once a month or once in six weeks and rubber can only be tapped in dry weather - when it rains the work has to stop. Pepper can only be harvested 30 months after first planting, and the best crops do not appear until the seventh year. Between sowing and reaping dry padi grows for about 100 days. Thus both landholders and labourers in the rural districts experience slack times when they almost inevitably find themselves badly in need of ready money.

Roughly speaking, all the inhabitants of the rural districts may be divided into two classes: the shopkeepers and the planters. The relations between these two classes are based upon an elaborate system of credit (described in detail below) which is necessitated in part by the seasonal nature of agricultural work, but much more by the extreme lack of capital among the rural planters. In effect, the shopkeepers, owning some capital, act as loan making capitalists and bankers, while the planters, having none, constitute a labour force in their employ.

Since the general standard of living is so low, there is very little difference to be observed within each category. All the labourers do the same work, all the shops sell the same goods. It may not be out of place here to quote a description of the old type of Chinese shop - they have not altered much in the rural bazaars :

"When I first knew Sarawak practically every Chinese Bazaar was an exact copy of every other except in size. The days of plate glass windows, show cases and English speaking shop assistants had not arrived. The same goods were stocked in the same way - - rather higgledy-piggledy to our lights -- but according to a system of their own. Boxes of rice, carefully graded according to quality. Tubs of various pastes, all rather smelly but undoubtedly good - - pickled eggs of some antiquity, strings of vermicelli, exotic looking Chinese dried fruits, layers and layers of salt fish, salt, sugar, bits of shark, birdsnests; all these foods which the people love. Behind were bales of calico, that unbleached cloth known as "blachu", dark blue cotton, bright red cotton. Bundles of cheap flowered cloths, imitation "Batik" sarongs and butter muslin. Straw hats, sock suspenders, purse belts, singlets, made-up bow ties and hair ribbons. Tiger balm, camphor oil, Dr. Williams' Pink Pills, and vaseline. Tin plates, kettles, clogs and pocket knives - - what a collection! - - -but all desirable to the people. Candidly, I don't know how all these shops carried it all. Then of course the ways of Chinese commerce are a mystery to us. In a small town you might get twenty or thirty of these shops, all the same and all receiving custom."[2]

It is clear that the rural districts in Sarawak suffer peculiar difficulties. The lack of transport alone is sufficient to explain economic back-

---

1. The problem of the disposal of local produce is described in a later chapter.
2. J.B. Archer, Autobiography. Unpublished M.S.

wardness, while the standard of living is further affected by the seasonal nature of agricultural employment and the lack of alternative occupations. In a community where economic conditions are well-developed, the elaboration of the division of labour produces occupation organisations, such as guilds and trade unions, and the frequency of individual contacts produces voluntary organisations, such as clubs. This has happened everywhere among urban Chinese overseas. But in the rural districts of Sarawak economic conditions are obviously still in too rudimentary a state of development for organisations of this kind. Apart from the bonds of kinship and of dialect similarity there exist no other sufficiently distinctive relationships which could be used for the purposes of social organisation. The situation in this respect is essentially similar to that in rural China, and as a consequence the social structure of the rural Chinese communities in Sarawak is also essentially similar to that of rural China. Social bonds in rural China are bonds of 'blood' and geographical neighbourhood. Now we have already seen that in Sarawak even in the urban areas grouping by dialect similarity really amounts to an assertion of solidarity among people who derive from the same original neighbourhood in the Chinese homeland, while clanship among the urban Chinese of Sarawak, though differing in details of organisation fulfills much the same role. The Chinese of Sarawak were nearly all rural farmers in the original Chinese homeland and they continue to organise themselves in terms of the ideals of local solidarity that were valid for the Chinese context. The contrast in Sarawak between the organisation of the urban and the rural Chinese is not explainable therefore in terms of difference of original background. Likewise the similarity between rural China and the rural Sarawak is not a mere transplantation of traditional ways of life, but an outcome of similar economic conditions.

Clan relationships also function as an essential part of the machinery of immigration. Chinese immigration into the Nan Yang is everywhere a matter of private enterprise and personal endeavour. The immigration regulations require that each new arrival should have an entry permit issued by the Immigration Office in the Colony. Visas are now also required for transit through Hong Kong (except for Cantonese) and Singapore, and are only granted by the British Consulates in China on production of the necessary entry permit. Thus a prospective entrant must have his permit before he leaves home, and as it can only be obtained from the colony itself he must have a contact there to apply for him. The actual application is nearly always made by a close kinsman -- parent, spouse, or offspring -- of the immigrant, usually with the help of other clansmen.[1]

---

1. There are also specially created travel agencies, with branches at strategic points both in the Nan Yang and in China (and especially in Hong Kong), whose services and advice can be obtained. At one time certain of these agencies used to hand out permits in China, but these were forged and the agencies suffered a decline. Since the depression immigration has been increasingly restricted until to-day it is almost at a standstill. Permits are issued very sparingly, usually only to bona fide wives of settlers, their young children, or labourers of a type for which there is a positive demand. This restriction obviously contributes further to the decline of the agencies. Now-a-days every immigrant relies upon clan and locality contacts. The agencies survive, however: the Thomas Cooks of the Far East. They have chains of hotels, catering for each dialect group, at places of transit, and for payment of a lump sum, will provide for the transport and board of travellers. There are, for example four Hakka "kheh chang" in Kuching, besides three ordinary Chinese hotels. A similar system obtains within China itself.
Besides the agencies there are also free lance professional travellers (shui kheh) who travel between China and the Nan Yang taking goods, letters, remittances, and often acting as guides for individuals, particularly women and children. Ordinary experienced travellers, returning to China or the Nan Yang, are often asked to accompany others, as well as to take goods, letters, etc. in much the same way. The 'shui kheh' are paid a regular commission.
The policies of the shipping companies, too, have an influence on the flow of immigrants. By reducing or increasing the fares, or granting special facilities to 'shui kheh', for example, a shipping company may play quite a large part. The standing of the different companies, and their connections both with the Chinese agencies and with the Immigration authorities, are also relevant factors. For example, if a reputable company can guarantee direct transit through Singapore it may not be necessary for the passengers to obtain visas.
Editorial note: It must be stressed again that the author is writing of conditions as he found them in 1949.

Entry permits are only issued to those whose future occupation and ability to maintain themselves are guaranteed both by the applicant on behalf of the new immigrant, and by a formal guarantor acting on behalf of one of the recognised dialect Associations. We shall see later who these eminent citizens tend to be, but in any case it is one of the immigrant's clansmen who makes the contact with the formal guarantor. Thus it is clear that no new immigrant can enter the Colony unless he already has contacts there, and that he inevitably relies largely upon his own clansmen and members of his own dialect group.

The willingness of settlers to make immigration arrangements for their kinsmen is likely to vary with varying conditions in Sarawak and in China. At a time of expanding trade or production, when labour is required, it is an asset to bring in more immigrants, but at a time of recession further dependents are a burden. During the Sino-Japanese war large numbers of men anxious to escape conscription at home left for the Nan Yang with the help of relatives who shared the traditional Chinese disdain for the soldier's life.

In the rural districts the rather informal, none the less real, clan organisation described in the preceding chapter and mentioned here in connexion with channels of immigration is of abiding social and economic significance to the individual. For example, when a new immigrant arrives he has to pass through a period of "being a new boy" (Sinkheh). To the difficulties of physical acclimatisation to the tropics are added difficulties of social and psychological adjustment, as well, of course, as difficulties of getting started in a new job. It is his co-clan members who give the new immigrant help in these early, and crucial, days. In the old days (even as recently as five years ago) it was the custom for each new immigrant to ask someone (usually a kinsman) to be his "guardian". The newcomer worked for his guardian in return for his meals, a small sum for pocket money and minute instruction in the ways of his new, tropical, life. The guardian also acted as a caretaker for any property or money the newcomer might have. During this period, which usually lasted for at least six months, the "new boy" began to learn the new skills he would require in order to get a livelihood -- jungle clearing, rubber tapping, for example -- and the hygienic habits which the overseas Chinese have acquired through long years of tropical experience.[1] After this period of probation most of the new immigrants were able to set up more or less independently, with the help of influence of their guardians; or they might continue to work for their guardians, but now in return for wages. Apart from his co-clan members there was no one at all to whom a new immigrant might turn for help. To-day this system of guardianship is not so strictly adhered to, but clan relationships still remain the rallying points, as it were, around which the overseas Chinese congregate.

The vast majority of new immigrants have always arrived in Sarawak with empty pockets. With no capital to start with, new arrivals struggle to accumulate savings as well as to provide for their daily bread. But, as we have seen, neither rubber nor padi cultivation can provide constant employment or a constant income. Thus, as all savings made at a time of maximum employment are used up during the slack or bad seasons, rural workers cannot build up any capital reserve. Living right up to the hilt of one's income like this is the best that can happen. At the worst, when rubber prices are falling or the price of foodstuffs rising, dependence upon credit is the only alternative to destitution.

The average size of rubber holdings in Sarawak is small. Malay and Dayak holdings average 1·45, Chinese 5·81 acres.[2] From such minute patches a minute return is all that can be expected. Even the few larger holdings[3] are not

---

1. We have already seen (p.9 above) that according to the traditional ways a new immigrant must have seven cold showers a day, and the way of taking these is carefully prescribed. In addition methods of preventing sun-stroke, avoiding and treating influenza and so forth are taught.
2. Statistics of Rubber Holdings. (Office of Rubber Control. Sarawak.) 1941.
3. There are only 44 holdings of more than 100 acres in the whole Colony. 28 of these are in the First Division. Ibid.
   Returns might be better with better management, but "the general standard of technique of management, tapping, and of sheet manufacture of the small holders is very low indeed". Sarawak Department of Agriculture. Annual Report for 1947. (Kuching 1948) p.3 #23

much more remunerative. For example, one Chinese rubber planter near Kuching holds 77 acres of rubber land. On this he employs Malay labourers, three married couples and four bachelors, to whom he pays piece rates. This planter's gross monthly income, from rubber, works out at about $419.56, out of which he has to pay about $297.12 in wages etc. This leaves him with an average net monthly income of $122.44, and with the further income which he obtains from the sale of fish from ponds on his estate he is able to live in a shop-house and send all his four children to school. At the same time, however, his wife has to work, and the rubber yields are only obtained by the most economical, not to say actully cruel, methods of management.[1]

The ordinary small-holder, employing no hired labour, is in considerably worse case. Let us take the case of a family consisting of a man, wife and three male children (aged 14, 12 and 5 years) and holding 5 acres of rubber.[2] The two elder children help their parents on the holding for several hours each day before going to school. The planter reckons that in a good month he can make about $75, and in a poor month about $50. To set against this he gives the following details of monthly expenditure :-

	$. c.
Rice	30.00
Coffee	2.00
Milk (tinned)	3.00
Vegetables (approx.)	4.50
Meat (approx.)	6.00
Cooking fat	4.00
Kerosene	4.00
School fees	7.50
Salt	0.50
Other condiments	1.00
Soap	1.75
	62.75

There is also intermittently recurrent necessary expenditure on school-uniform and textbooks. Obviously in a slack month this budget simply does not balance,[3] while even in a good month there are hardly more than $12 over for such things as clothing, cigarettes, rice wine, or any form of literature or entertainment.[4] Kerosene, soap and school fees are the only non-food items in the above list. Food accounts for 78·7% of the total expenditure.

It is not easy to generalise about the economic position of the hired labourer to-day, partly because owing to the labour shortage the turnover is remarkably rapid and partly because conditions of employment vary considerably. Very often an agricultural labourer shares the product on a 50:50 basis, thus receiving about $25 - $35 a month. In addition he is provided with accommodation, and often eats with the small-holder's family but pays for his food. A labourer who receives a regular wage instead of a 50:50 share, usually gets about $15 - $22 a month, with similar living and feeding arrangements. Nowa-

---

1. For comparison of living standards: the lower grade European civil servant in Sarawak receives $450 per mensem, plus cost of living allowances.

2. This information was gathered at a group interview at which the investigator discussed family budgeting with 37 family heads, all of the T'iens. Points put forward by one man were commented upon by the others, and in this way a rough estimate of common experience was gained.

3. For example in May 1949 there were 27 days of rain, during which no rubber tapping could be carried out at all.

4. In Sembera some old people complained sadly of the "extravagance" of these modern days. The Travelling Cinema comes just twice a year, and tickets cost 30 cents, 50 cents and 70 cents. "Regular cinema going" cleans up all the family savings.

days few small-holders can afford to employ labour even at this wage.[1]   The custom of sharing the family meals makes it difficult to estimate the expenditure of hired labourers. A man living alone and cooking for himself might exist at the following minimum standard[2] :-

	$. c.
Rice	11.25
Sugar	1.48
Coffee	0.50
Dried fish	1.00
Meat	2.50
Vegetables	1.00
Salt	0.15
Other condiments	0.50
Kerosene	1.20
Soap	0.70
Cigarettes	1.50
	21.83

In such circumstances as these it is not difficult to understand how the whole economic structure of the rural areas comes to be built up on a system of credit. Some of the ways in which this system actually works may now be described.

Some Chinese immigrants became debtors before ever they reached Sarawak. They were those who came under contract to work for a certain employer for a predetermined number of years. The employers paid their passage money and provided the immigrants with accommodation, food and a little pocket money. A man who could repay the passage money could free himself from his contract to work; but very few were ever in a position to do this. The pocket money was always completely insufficient, and therefore the immigrants had to borrow — from their employers. To the original debt for passage money which was paid off by contract labour, was now added a financial debt usually to the same creditor. Such contracts as these are unlawful, and no cases of this sort have been brought to the attention of the authorities since the close of the Japanese war.

The prohibition of gambling houses has also done a good deal to help this class of debtor. Previously most of them used to try to improve their position by gambling, and thus only fell deeper into debt.

After the period of being a "new boy" described above, the ordinary Chinese immigrant in the rural areas nearly always desires to obtain his own piece of land in order to set up as an independent cultivator - that is, of course, if he be free to do so and not bound by any contract. The problem then is how is he to get his land without any initial capital? Even if he is able to get land through Government channels, his problem remains acute. It will take him a whole year to open up the virgin jungle before he can begin even to plant. How is he to secure the necessities of life during this time without money? Money cannot be his before his first harvest - perhaps several years ahead. He is forced to borrow.

Loans are supplied by the shops. In the rural areas these are closely tied into the system of clan relationships. For example, in any rural district where are large number of members of a single clan are congregated, there will be found shops owned by members of that clan. These are always the shopping centres of the other co-clan members. The T'ien clan is only a small group in comparison with some really large Hoppu Hakka clans, but in the First Division

---

1. Urban wages, as is usual, are higher. Government claims that "50% of the shop-assistants in Kuching receive more than $50 a month, and all receive free food and lodging or allowance of $30 in lieu. The wharf labourers claim to have a monthly budget of $206.30 on an average (for a family of 5½ persons). They may earn as much as $260 a month. Bus drivers get $120 a month or more."
2. See footnote 2   p. 40.

there are no less than eleven shops owned by T'ien clan members, covering all the bazaar centres where members of the T'ien clan are to be found. In the second Division there are three T'ien owned shops, in the Third Division five and in the Fourth Division two. Each of these shops is well known to all members of the clan, not simply to those who live in the same district, so that wherever a T'ien clan member may go he can obtain help and information from his own clansmen's shops. In Siniawan there are two shops owned by members of the T'ien clan.[1] There are 54 T'ien families in that area, of which 45 are regular customers at one of these two shops and 6 at the other (the majority of whose clients are Dayaks). Only 3 T'ien families shop at establishments owned by members of other clans.

In the rural districts actual money loans are far less frequent than in Kuching or the bigger bazaar centres. Only the biggest bazaar shops can afford to lend out money in advance, allowing the borrower to pay back in rural produce afterwards. The rural shops are, as a rule, carried on with very limited capital, and it is impossible for them to take the risk of advancing money in this way. In the towns a borrower whose credit is good is usually asked to pay 2% - 3% interest per month, but a countryman is hardly likely to be accepted as a debtor at so low a rate.[2] The most usual rate is about 4% per month, but higher rates are not uncommon.[2] It is interesting to note that credit transactions in money are often carried out between members of different clans, and, indeed, it is sometimes even stated that it is better for such transactions to take place between members of different dialect groups. It is easy to see how the mutual sentiments of clan relationship may affect the business interests both of the debtor, who wants to make as good a bargain as possible, and of the creditor, who may need to apply drastic measures to get his money back.

Lack of capital in the rural shops often means that the cash actually borrowed by rural Chinese has passed through the hands of at least three different money lenders, the rate of interest increasing at each step from, say, 2½% to 7%. In Siniawan and elsewhere one can find several examples of comparatively well-to-do money-lenders who have been able to borrow money from the banks at 2½% per month, probably against mortgage; from this they have lent to the shops at about 3% - 3½% per month, while the shops in their turn are lending to the peasants at 4% or 5% per month. In a developed economy money can be borrowed from branch banks away from the city centres of population, because the financial position of the borrower is strong enough for them to be able to give security, in some form of property. In Sarawak, however, the only Chinese people who can give this kind of impersonal security are the well-to-do traders and dealers in Kuching and one or two other centres. The banks do not develop rural branches because it is not worth their while to do so. The rural peasant, having no property, has only his good name to offer as security. But this personal kind of security will only be accepted by his clansmen. Hence the necessity for the rural Chinese to depend upon clan relationships for their economic position, even for their very subsistence.

The undeveloped state of the rural districts of Sarawak and the generally very low standard of living mean that cash transactions are, however, rare in these districts. The credit system is mainly carried on in goods. Creditor shops advance daily provisions in return for agricultural produce. That is why Sarawak is so full of grocery shops, nearly every one of which sells the same kind of provisions. Each peasant family keeps a small note book in which the shopkeeper with whom it deals writes down a credit and debit account of rubber (or other produce) against groceries. The account is always kept in money values; there is no question of barter.

Because of the different harvesting periods of rubber, on the one hand, and padi or pepper, on the other, there are differences between the methods by which rubber planters and padi or pepper farmers obtain their groceries on credit. The former exist on what might perhaps be called a series of short term loans with payment by instalments, whereas the latter obtains comparatively

---

1. Two shops out of a total of twenty-eight in the area as a whole.
2. The highest rate discovered by the investigator was paid by a man who had borrowed $100 on the understanding that in 3 months' time he would repay $150.

long term loans.

As we have seen, nearly every rural Chinese deals with his own clansmen's shops. Rubber planters who have a long standing connexion with the shop simply send their rubber sheets in, almost every afternoon, often by the children, trusting the shopkeeper to write down the correct current price. Others may spend a longer time each day ascertaining the current price and making sure that it is correctly entered. In either case the next daily step is to order the daily grocery supplies - from the same shop. If all goes well, the value of the rubber brought in may be just enough to cover the cost of necessities, if not each day, then at least over a reasonably short period. It is the usual practice for these Chinese rubber planters to rely upon their rubber for the supply of foodstuffs, kerosene and so forth, and to purchase other goods and services, such as school fees, uniforms, clothing, with the cash received from pig and poultry breeding. Once the pig, or the fowl, is taken to market and sold the money is usually spent almost at once, so, if the rubber yield is low, or if a prolonged period of rain or sickness prevents regular work, the planter has no savings to fall back upon, but simply finds himself dropping further and further behind on the instalment payments of his debts. Through a long process of accumulation it has now become established that by paying off only a portion of his outstanding debt a regular client can always get further provisions on credit. As the average rubber holding is small and the price of rubber low, a client can almost never pay off the whole debt, and so the process of accumulation continues, while the evil day of reckoning is staved off as long as possible.

Figures collected in 1949 from three rural bazaar centres in the First Division give some indication of the scale of this rural credit system. At one point along the Simanggang Road there are about 15 shops. Most of these are small, single line establishments, but 7 are fairly large grocery-cum-rubber-dealer stores. Of these the 3 most recently opened have each about $2,000 out on loan, 4 others between $4,000 and $6,000, and one, the largest and oldest (it was opened about 20 years ago, and many of its clients must have returned to China or left the district or died, long since) claims an outstanding loan of about $7,000. In a certain bazaar in the Bau area there are a dozen grocer-dealers. Six of them claim to have advanced goods to the value of between $4,000 and $5,000, five $5,000, and one, the largest, a Fukienese shop, as much as $10,000. In one coastal bazaar the majority of the 20 grocer-dealers stated in 1949 that they had advanced between $1,000 and $2,000 worth of goods, but 2 claimed $8,000 and the largest, a Teochow, stated himself that he was owed as much as $15,000.[1]

The amounts owed to the shops by individual debtors range in value from about $50 to about $2,000. The distribution of debts owed to one particular shop in the Bau area is as follows :-

Amount owed $	Number of debtors
40 - 50	9
51 - 100	15
101 - 200	21
201 - 300	24
301 - 400	9
401 - 500	2
501 - 600	1
601 - 800	2

The rural Chinese who wants to plant pepper or padi can ask for long term credit. There are always a few relatively more wealthy shop-owners or money-lenders in the rural areas who are willing to render this service to planters whose crops have a seasonal harvest, and also to rubber planters when they first set up on their own without capital to tide them over the initial growing

1. All these figures were collected by direct questioning of shopkeepers. It is possible that an element of boasting has led to exaggeration in certain cases. Other shopkeepers in the coastal bazaar, for example, did not share the Teochow shopkeeper's estimate of his own debt, but suggested it was probably about 1/3 or 1/2 smaller.

period. Credit is obtained in this way on condition that the debtor makes an extra payment of 30% in addition to a monthly interest of 2% which is charged on any debt lasting longer than a year. In practice what happens is that the shopkeeper debits the planter's account with the price of each article   purchased plus 30%. The 2% monthly interest is payable on the total debt.   In the old days this was considered the normal arrangement for planters to make, but as nowadays most of the actual working planters of padi and pepper are employed by absentee landlords few of them now get credit on these terms.

At first sight this credit system appears to be very unfair to the peasants and labourers. In actual fact, however, it is the inevitable outcome of the peculiar economic and environmental circumstances of rural Sarawak.   The small size of the holdings and of the labour units working them, and the great difficulties of transport, as well as the lack of capital, make any other system out of the question at present. If a small rubber holder were to transport all his crop to a big bazaar centre for sale, he would never be able to afford the transport fee, while his absence would jeopardise the whole working of the small (usually family) labour group. Moreover we have already shown how it is impossible for the small peasant, unknown and without security, to borrow from the banks; so in the big bazaars he would still be without credit.

In the rural areas the peasants have at least some methods of escape. They can, for instance, simply disappear. This is not uncommon, for one can easily go to N. Borneo, Brunei or Dutch territory, or lose oneself in the large population of Miri. A certain Hakka come to settle near Nonok in 1949,   and opened up a patch of land on which to grow beans. Beans take three months before harvest, and during the first three months this peasant drew his goods on credit from the rural store in the usual way. By the time he had accumulated a debt of $70 the three months were over - but his bean crop was a total failure. First he sent his wife and children away; then he just vanished himself. In Nonok, too, many peasants were avoiding their difficulties in 1948 by transferring their custom to different shops. The majority of the shops in Nonok are concentrated in one bazaar street. About half a mile outside the settlement there are five separate stores. If the peasants went into the bazaar they would inevitably meet their creditors and the value of their produce would simply go towards the payment of their old debts. If they wanted cash, or if they wanted to open a new account, they would go to one of the outlying shops, all of which were doing such a flourishing trade in 1948 that the bazaar shopowners reported to the D.O. demanding that they be compelled to come into the bazaar area.[1] A third method of escape is known by a phrase meaning "through the back door", because when a peasant cannot pay his debt he can always take his produce to another shop by the back door, and so avoid meeting his creditor in front of his own shop.

Thus it is not only the peasants who are in difficulties. The rural shopkeepers, too, are faced by an apparently insoluble dilemma. They cannot afford to go on lending in this way, but they can do nothing else either, for only by allowing credit in return for part payment can they hope to get any return at all. At the same time, however, the peasants are not free to do exactly as they like. Their attachment to the land and their ties of clanship act as a brake. A man is desparately anxious to keep his land, and even more anxious to keep "face" before his kinsmen. He is, therefore, unlikely to let his creditors down completely. The shopkeepers feel that they can accept the risk of abscondment by an occasional bad debtor.

This mutual interdependence of creditor and debtor is further proven by the existence of the high rates of interest already mentioned. Very high interest rates usually point to a rather peculiar relationship between creditor and debtor. The creditor knows that the debtor cannot earn enough to pay the interest, and knows that he cannot get both capital and interest paid back. However, the debtor also knows this, and he exploits the creditor just as the creditor exploits him. The creditor can never foreclose on his bad debt, and as the debtor is aware of this he therefore only goes on paying up so long as

---

1. Under the Rural Bazaar Ordinance which states that all shop-houses must be built of wood, not atap, and on land allocated by Government.

45

it is to his advantage to do so, that is so long as the creditor appears willing to continue advancing further credit. In purely economic terms, then, the Chinese rural shopkeepers and peasants in Sarawak are mutually interdependent. This economic interdependence is fortified by the mutual clan interrelationships which make the credit system fluently workable. Because co-clan members know each other and are prepared to vouch for each other, it is not necessary to offer security against a debt or to produce any other guarantee of repayment.

Bonds of clanship also tend to mitigate the harshness of the economic situation for both shopkeepers and peasants. We have seen how but for clanship the credit system in the rural areas, upon which both depend, would not work at all. But clan ties do more than provide the framework for the working of the rural economy. Clan relationships have an ultimate, irreducible value of their own. A good turn to a co-clan member compensates, in part at least, for economic loss. One may lose money, but one acquires merit, and, above all, "face". Early in 1949 a certain shopkeeper in Seniawan received a call from his classificatory uncle, a peasant, who had come to bid him goodbye before going away to try to improve his fortunes elsewhere. It turned out that the older man owed his clansman $90. It also turned out that he was unable to meet the debt, and, indeed, could not even produce the necessary $2. for his launch ticket. The nephew put his hand in his pocket - thus increasing his total loss to $92. "But", as he said with a shrug "what else could I do? He is my kinsman."

VII

O C C U P A T I O N A L   I D E N T I F I C A T I O N   A N D   B A Z A A R   E C O N O M Y

The urban bazaar centres, like Kuching, Sibu and Semanggang, present an essentially different problem from that posed by the rural districts. The very nature of the small-holding agricultural work which is characteristic of the latter tends to ensure the continued isolation of the rural families, which is further increased by the notoriously poor development of communications. Relations with the outside world are virtually confined to the necessities of getting daily nourishment, and contacts for purposes of marriage and so forth In these circumstances kinship bonds appear to be the most convenient framework for social relations, and individual families are linked together almost solely by the network of clan and affinal ties. Links with the outside world do exist, but only indirectly - through the bazaars. In the urban environment, however, the problem of communications does not arise. On the contrary, individuals from other families are easily accessible, while the nature of the bazaar economy forces contacts with others, not only within the bazaar itself, but in other divisions and even in the great world beyond the sea.

Moreover, in further contrast to the rural areas the population of which is, as we have seen, predominantly drawn from one single dialect group, the bazaars contain speakers of many different dialects living side by side. Thus, whereas in describing the rural economy we were dealing with the social relations between largely isolated families within one dialect group, in the towns we are dealing with relations between individuals of different dialect groups, and between one dialect group and another. It is therefore clear that in both economic and social terms the urban, bazaar economy presents a very different picture from that of the rural areas, and we must expect the structure of social relations to be different too.

The bazaar areas are the most overcrowded parts of the towns.[1] The usual shop-house buildings which are characteristic of all this part of the Far East are tightly packed together along the streets - in Semanggang about 42 only,

1. Measured by H.M. Ministry of Health Standards (1937) more than 76 families in the bazaar area are living in overcrowded conditions. See my Report on Over-Crowding in Kuching (1949). Typescript. (on file in Secretariat, Kuching).

in Sibu 132 and in Kuching more than 500. Kuching streets are thronged with shoppers at almost all times of day from dawn to dusk, and the back streets even later - wooden heels on the cement paving, bicycle bells, shouts, white shirts, bright sarongs, all the noise and colour of the East Indies. Most of the business is carried on in the shop-houses themselves, but there are a few street hawkers selling cigarettes and cooked foods from stalls. Almost every shop is Chinese owned; a few Malay shops are quite unimportant and the European firms deal in wholesale business only. There are, however, quite a number of Indian shops dealing mainly in materials and clothes.[1] There tends to be a concentration of types of shop: generally speaking the road parallel to the river, Old Bazaar Street, contains grocery stores; Indian Street, Carpenter Street and Yeau Hai Street contain general stores; hardware merchants and goldsmiths congregate in Upper Rock Street, tinsmiths in China Street and so forth. Coffee shops and bicycle stores are scattered everywhere amongst the others. As we shall see later this concentration of certain types of business, incomplete as it is, implies also a tendency towards the local concentration of members of the same dialect group.

Each Chinese shop is an independent unit. An analysis of the nature of shop ownership makes this quite clear. The total number of businesses and shops in Kuching in 705.[2] Of these 455 (that is, 64·6%) are separately owned by single individual owners. Another 151 (21·4%) are held each in partnership between two members of a single dialect group, while in addition to these there are 57 (8%) which are shared between members of the same family.[3] Shops shared by partners who speak different dialects are only 42 in number (6%) and of these 16 (2·3%) are on premises in which manufacturing work, for example cycle and machine workshops, boatbuilding, printing, is carried out, and 26 (3·7%) are purely commercial concerns. The following Table gives the details of these figures :-

T A B L E   10

OWNERSHIP   OF   CHINESE   SHOPS   IN   KUCHING

Dialect Group	Single Owner	Partners of Same Dialect Group	Partners of Same Family[3]	Total
Teochow	135	58	14	207 (29.4%)
Fukien	131	35	7	173 (24·5%)
Hakka	84	28	13	125 (17·7%)
Henghua	46	14	7	67 (9·6%)
Chao An	6	2	3	11 (1·5%)
Foochow	5	6	2	13 (1·8%)
Cantonese	36	7	7	50 (7·0%)
Hainan	10	1	4	15 (2·1%)
Luichow	1			
Other Groups	1			
TOTAL :	455 (64·6%)	151 (21·4%)	57 (8%)	663 (94%)*

* The remaining 42 (6%) are shared by partners of different dialect groups.

1. The power of "Indians" and "Arabs" in the textile trade seems general in the Moslem Indies. Perhaps the fact that they deal in sarongs, which are a style of dress peculiar to the Indies and still largely manufactured by traditional Indian methods may help to explain why in this field alone the Chinese do not predominate.
2. The material for this and the following paragraphs is drawn from the files of the Registrar's Office in Kuching. Every shop has to be licensed, and when the licence is granted full particulars of ownership are taken. Records were started in 1935. If a shop goes out of business, however, the fact is not always reported; at the same time not every licence taken out implies the definite existence of a separate shop - as a result the figures given in the text may not reflect the actual situation with complete accuracy.
3. This sharing is not strictly a question of legal "partnership", but indicates a common interest by, for example, two brothers, in the same business. The term 'family' here refers to close kin of the same household such as: brothers, father and son, uncle and nephew or husband and wife.

It can thus be seen that shop-keeping in Kuching is carried on by a large number of small separate concerns, each usually exclusive to the members of one dialect group. For example, 107 (15.7%) of the shops employ no assistants at all, business being entirely in the hands of the owners' families; 523 (73·5%) shops employ assistants from the same dialect groups as their owners, and only 75 (10·6%) engage assistants from some other dialect group. This social exclusiveness can also be illustrated from a consideration of marriage arrangements. In these 705 shops there are 1,509 married couples. Of these only 212 (14%) comprise man and wife of different dialect groups or race;[1] all the others (1,297, or 86%) are marriages between speakers of the same dialect.

The dialect exclusiveness exhibited by individual shops in Kuching is a concomitant of the phenomenon which we have already briefly referred to in Chapter IV as "occupational identification". The following Table gives a detailed analysis of the way in which members of the same dialect group tend to be concentrated in the same business :-

TABLE 11 - overleaf.

---

1. Data from the field material gathered in the course of the 1946-7 Census of Sarawak. In 78 cases Chinese men have married Malay or Dayak wives. It is probable that in the outstations the rate of cross-cultural marriage is much higher.

T A B L E

RELATIONSHIP BETWEEN DIALECT SIMILARITY AND

	1✝	2✝	3✝	4*	5✝	6✝	7*	8✝
	Clock & watch Shops	Tin-smiths	Carpen-ters	Fisher-men	Bicycle Shops	Tailors	Coffee Shops	Veget-able retail-
Hainan						4 (8·7%)	171 (78·8%)	
Henghua				253 (96%)	27 (84%)			
Hakka		14 (100%)				36 (78·3%)	7 (3·2%)	51 (70%)
Fukien					3 (10%)		10 (4·6%)	10 (13%)
Teochow					1 (3%)	1 (2·2%)	6 (2·8%)	5 (7%)
Luichow							1 (0·4%)	
Cantonese	7 (100%)					5 (10·8%)	6 (2·8%)	3 (6%)
Chao An								
Foochow				10 (4%)	1 (3%)		16 (7·4%)	2 (4%)
Southern Mandarin			15 (100%)					
Malays & Dayaks								

* Figures of membership of occupational Associations

✝ Figures of business owners.

11.

OCCUPATIONAL GROUPING IN KUCHING (1948 - 1949)

9/	10*	11/	12/	13/	14/	15*	16*	17/	18*
Shoe-makers	Rubber exporters	Char-coal makers	Chinese druggists	Gold-smiths	Con-tractors	Wharf labourers	Grocers	Barbers	Bus Drivers
							3 (1·5%)		
							5 (2·6%)	3 (16·6%)	34 (35·4%)
1 (20%)	1 (5%)	2 (18·2%)	7 (53·8%)	2 (8%)	1 (1·5%)	10 (3%)	25 (13·1%)	7 (38·8%)	37 (38·6%)
	11 (55%)	1 (9%)		12 (59%)	2 (3%)	37 (11·2%)	63 (33·1%)		4 (4·2%)
1 (20%)	8 (40%)	2 (18.2%)	5 (38·4%)	4 (19%)	1 (1·5%)	87 (26·3%)	73 (38·9%)		7 (7·3%)
		6 (54·6%)				2 (0·6%)			
3 (60%)			1 (10·8%)	3 (14%)		1 (0·3%)	5 (2·6%)	4 (22·3%)	
					5 (8%)	142 (43·3%)	13 (6·8%)		12 (12·5%)
					8 (3%)		3 (1·5%)	2 (4%)	
					46 (73%)				2 (2%)

The figures for this Table are of two kinds: those marked with an asterisk (*) refer to the membership of registered occupational Associations, they were collected from the registration books of each Association; those marked with a dagger (≠) refer to the owners of businesses, the employers, and were collected during a house to house survey conducted by the writer in 1948-9.The difference becomes significant in certain cases: for example,in certain businesses where, as we shall see, a new division between employers and employees is becoming clear, or in certain trades, such as the goldsmiths, the charcoal makers and some others where the employers are of one dialect group and the skilled workers of another. In these cases the figures in this Table appear definitely misleading, for the actual goldsmiths and charcoal makers are Cantonese and Luichow people respectively, the Fukienese are simply capitalist employers.

The Table clearly shows that in every business there is a single dominating dialect group. In certain cases this dominance is absolute: all the clock and watch shops are Cantonese,[1] all the tinsmiths are Hakka speaking,[2] all the carpenters speak a southern dialect of Mandarin (indeed, they all come from the same village in Southern Kiangsi). 96% of the fishermen are from Henghua, and so are 84%of the owners of bicycle shops. 78% of the tailors and 70% of the sellers of vegetables are Hakkas. The coffee shops are 78 Hainanese, and the goldsmiths 59% Fukienese. Three out of the five shoemakers are Cantonese, and six out of the eleven charcoal makers are from the Luichow peninsula. In none of these occupations do speakers of other dialects even begin to approach the numbers of the dominant dialect group.

The remaining eight occupations listed here (rubber exporter,Chinese drugstore keeper, goldsmith, contractor, wharf-labourer, grocer, barber and bus driver) are also each predominantly associated with a particular dialect group, though,in each, other groups also have a significant place.In most cases, however, the number of dialect groups associated with the particular job in question is limited, and what has happened is simply a joint specialisation in one occupation by two or more dialect groups. This is true of the big rubber exporters, for instance, of whom 11 (55%) are Fukienese and 8 (40%)are Teochows. It is also true of the Hakka and Teochow specialisation in Chinese drugs. Both these occupations are found in similar dialect hands in Singapore. The position of the last five occupations listed (contractors, wharf-labourers,grocers, barbers and bus drivers) is somewhat different. 73% of the contractors are not Chinese at all. Of the Chinese contractors,while eight are Foochow speaking, five are Chao An who are able to compete with the richer Foochows because owing to the large Chao An settlement in Kuching, they can easily find labourers from their own dialect group. The Chao An dominance in wharf labour before the war has already been mentioned, and so has the fact that the influx of other groups is recent - Teochows approach most nearly to the Choa An group in this occupation, but wharf-labourers are to-day fairly well distributed throughout the Chinese community. Grocers, barbers and bus drivers might be expected to be fairly equally distributed also, for each provides a service which is equally and with regular frequency demanded by the members of every dialect group. Not unexpectedly, especially in view of the ramifications of the system of credit, a Chinese in Sarawak likes to deal with a grocer of his own dialect group:thus the distribution of grocers' shops among the different dialect groups in Kuching corresponds approximately to the distribution of the Chinese population among those same dialect groups. The barbers of a particular dialect group tend to be situated in streets which are predominately that dialect group's preserve, and the bus drivers drive their vehicles out into the countryside to the places in which members of their own group reside.

The association of dialect with occupation is also apparent in the Second and Third Divisions. In Semanggang there are representatives of five dialect groups; the relative members of which can be assessed approximately from the

---

1. From a single hsien, Chow-Chin, in Kwangtung.
2. Also from a single hsien, Tap'u (Tappu).

following figures of attendance at the local Chung Hwa School:

Teochow	174
Hakka	28
Hainan	17
Cantonese	7
Fukien	3
Indian, Dayak, Malay	8
Total :	237

There is a total of fifty-six shops in Semanggang. Thirty-four of them are grocers, 30 Teochow, 3 Hakka, 1 Cantonese. There are also 6 Hainan and 1 Teochow coffee shops, while the Teochows also provide 3 tailors, 2 restaurants, 2 "tooth artists", 1 photographer, 1 cinema and 1 Chinese druggist. Hakkas account for 2 barbers, 1 tinsmith and 1 wineshop, and Cantonese, in addition to the grocer already mentioned, 1 carpenter.[1]

In the larger Sibu the picture is more complex than in Semanggang. The total Chinese population of Sibu is 9,730, of whom nearly one third (i.e.3,068) are Foochow speakers. This Foochow preponderance reflects the rather peculiar distribution of Chinese dialect groups in the Third Division as a whole. It accounts for the large proportion of Foochow people to be found in almost every occupation in Sibu, though even there the tendency towards occupational identification is clearly observable. The following list makes this clear:

T A B L E 12

OCCUPATIONAL IDENTIFICATION IN SIBU (1948 - 1949)

Dialect Group

Occupation	Total No.	Foochow	Fukien	Cantonese	Henghua	Teochow	Hainan	Hakka
Tinsmiths	10	10 (100%)						
Taxidrivers	4				4 (100%)			
Bus-drivers	18	16			2			
Coffee shops	18	14		1			3	
Clock & watch shops	3	2	1					
Chinese drugs	10	5				1		4
Goldsmiths & silversmiths	15	10		5				
Bicycle shops	7	1			6			
General stores	15	9				6		
Grocers	39	21 (55%)	11			4		3
Wharf labourers*	232*	120*	94		18			

* Approximate figure: only 40 Foochow wharf labourers have actually joined the wharf labourers' Association in Sibu: it is estimated that there are about 80 others. Figures of wharf labour are therefore from the Association membership list plus an estimated further 80. Other figures here refer to shop owners only.

1. Figures refer to shop owners only.

Foochow people account for all the tinsmiths, and are also to be found in every other occupation except as taxidrivers - all four of whom are Henghua people. It is interesting to note this Henghua concentration in mechanical jobs which occurs even in this Foochow stronghold, as thoughout the Nan Yang. In a similar way Hainan people generally command the coffee shop business everywhere - and even in Sibu where there are only 162 Hainanese altogether as against the 3,608 Foochow people they run 3 out of the 18 coffee shops.[1] Again, although the numerically dominating Foochows run half the Chinese drug shops in Sibu, the usual Hakka and Teochow association with this business is also found there. At first sight the gold and silver smiths and clock and watch shops seem to show exceptions to the general picture of similar occupational identification in Kuching and elsewhere: the Foochow component is to be expected, owing, as his already been stressed, to the large numerical preponderance of these people in Sibu, but the association of Fukienese with clock and watch shops and of Cantonese with gold and silver smiths seems an exact reversal of the situation in Kuching where 100% of the clockshops are Cantonese and 59 of the goldsmiths Fukienese. It is here that the significance of the method of collecting the figures for these tables becomes apparent. These figures refer to the shop-owners, the employers. In Kuching the Fukienese "goldsmiths" employ Cantonese workers; at the same time it is worth noting that the biggest merchants of gold in Singapore are also Cantonese. The situation in Sibu is therefore quite in keeping. On the other hand the figures for clock and watch shops in Sibu also apply to employers only, the workers in these shops are Cantonese, and in this way they too agree with the general Nan Yang picture.[2]

The distribution of grocers' shops in Sibu, too, might almost have been predicted. The majority are Foochow owned, but 11 are Fukienese, the dialect group of second numerical importance in Sibu; 4 are Teochow, not actually the third largest group in Sibu, but a group everywhere particularly connected with the grocery business, and 3 are Hakka.[3] It is surprising that there are no Cantonese grocers' shops in Sibu, but even in Kuching where there are more than twice as many Cantonese people there are only 5 Cantonese grocers out of a total 192.

Description of business ownership in these three Sarawak towns, Kuching, Semanggang and Sibu, shows that there is a striking correlation between membership of a particular dialect group and connexion with a particular occupation. It is a correlation which is not absolute, however, and there are signs that it is tending to break down to-day. Generally speaking, occupational identification tends to be most complete where the occupation demands some special skill. The carpenters and tinsmiths of Kuching and Sibu are examples of this and so are the Kuching fishermen, tailors and shoemakers, the drug sellers and the workers in the clock and watch and gold and silver smiths' businesses. We have seen how in the last two cases the actual identification of dialect group with occupation is even more complete in practice than the tables here suggest. The same is true of charcoal making in Kuching. Table 11 shows that the majority of the charcoal makers are from Luichow, but in actual fact there are more Luichow charcoal makers than appear in the list; most of the Hakka, Fukien and Teochow "charcoal makers" are employers, for whom the skilled work is performed by paid Luichow labour. The skill required and carried by a particular dialect group may not be strictly a professional skill. For instance, Henghua people dominate most of the mechanical trades. The mechanical skills required are, of course, relatively new, in contrast to the long-standing tradition of charcoal making, and could be learnt by anyone: but the dominance of one dialect group means that the terms used in the trade belong to that one dialect. If a speaker of another dialect wishes to enter, say, the bicycle trade he must

---

1. 14 are Foochow owned. This may be linked not only with Foochow numerical preponderance in Sibu but also perhaps with the fact that Foochows rank second to Hainanese as coffee shop keepers in Kuching. See Table 11, p.48.
2. The majority of clock and watch shops in Singapore are in Cantonese hands, and Cantonese form the large majority of the membership of the clock and watch shop Association there.
3. Note how in Kuching the majority (39 , or 73 out of 192) of grocers' shops are Teochow, although these people are only second in numerical importance to the Hakka.

acquire not merely new mechanical but also new linguistic skills.[1]

An occupation which demands no special skill, and/or whose products are in constant, regular demand by all groups, is likely to be more widely distributed through the different dialect groups. The vegetable trade in Kuching, for example, is largely under Hakka dominance, but this is less because they have specially green fingers, than because Hakka (from Hweichow) form the majority of the farming and market-gardening population around Kuching. Members of at least four other dialect groups have a part in this trade. We have already mentioned the wide distribution of grocers, barbers and bus drivers.

The last, together with the wharf labourers, illustrate clearly the present tendency towards the breakdown of strict occupational identification. Neither occupation demands skills which are not easily acquired; both are widely distributed. Before the war, as we have seen, wharf labour was exclusively Chao An; to-day, members of six different groups are represented in its ranks. A bus driver is either an employee driving for a bus owning individual or company or else a part owner of his bus. In either case the capital is usually put up by either a Teochow or a Fukienese (occasionally a Hakka), nearly always a prosperous keeper of a grocery store, or a group of these. Here, then, is a counterpart to the case of the charcoal makers: among them the skilled work is mainly performed by a single dialect group, and capital is provided by Teochows or Fukienese, and sometimes Hakkas; for the bus drivers the work is less skilled, but capital is supplied by the same groups. It begins to look as if the occupation of "capitalist" itself may be identified with particular dialect groups.

The peculiar case of the coffee shop business requires special mention. The dominance of Hainanese in this trade has been stressed, but as Table 13 shows members of six other dialect groups are also engaged in it on a small scale. No special skill is required, and there is, of course, a regular demand for its services by members of all dialect groups. The figures for this trade were collected from the records of membership of the coffee shop associations. There are two of these, an employers' and an employees' association. The distribution of members can be shown thus :-

T A B L E   13

THE COFFEE SHOP BUSINESS

	Coffee Shops' Association (Employers)	Coffee and Teashop Employees' Association
Hainan	58 (66 %)	113 (88%)
Henghua	–	–
Hakka	4 (4·5%)	3 (2·1%)
Fukien	5 (5·7%)	5 (3·9%)
Teochow	6 (6·9%)	–
Luichow	1 (1·1%)	–
Cantonese	3 (3·3%)	3 (2·1%)
Chao An	–	–
Foochow	11 (12·5%)	5 (3·9%)
Southern Mandarin	–	–
Total :	88	129 217

The interesting thing to note here is that Hainan dominance is more marked among the employees than among the employers. Only 66% of the latter are Hainanese. Perhaps most significant is the Teochow group which consists of employers only. Once again we find an occupation in which, despite the clear predominance of a particular dialect group, the emergence of an employer class

1. In much the same way Hainanese terms abound in the coffee shop business. So much is this so that people shopping, say for cigarettes, nearly always ask for them in the Hainan dialect, no matter what their own native speech.

which does not necessarily belong to that group is apparent.

Employers can attain that position because they possess a relatively greater amount of capital. In some businesses occupational identification is simply connected with the control of capital. As we shall see later, the concentration of the rubber export trade in Fukien and Teochow hands is no accident, but is closely connected with the financial power of these two groups - a power which has several times been hinted at in the preceding paragraphs.

So far we have given a description of what might be called the vertical lines of occupational identification within each type of occupation. The economic activities of the bazaars, however, obviously require the development of relations between different types of occupation and, therefore, between different dialect groups. It is therefore necessary to consider the phenomenon of occupation identification as it is to be seen in the organisation of commercial relationships in Sarawak.

It is not proposed that the description of these relationships should deal in equal detail with every type of business activity. That would be tedious. Instead the following paragraphs concentrate mainly upon the grocery and rubber trades which may be described as the backbone of Chinese import and export in Sarawak. Rubber forms more than half of the total annual agricultural export from the Colony,[1] and groceries, or rather goods sold in general grocery stores,[2] are, as we have seen, the commodities in exchange for which rubber is primarily sold. Without exported rubber and imported groceries almost the whole of the Chinese population of the Colony would exist only at the level of subsistence agriculture - or, more probably, would be very considerably smaller than it is.

Grocery import and rubber export may, indeed, be regarded as obverse and reverse of one process. The system of credit which keeps the rural economy going depends, as we have seen, on the exchange of rubber for daily provisions. The rural grocery shops have a double function: as distributors of provisions and as collectors of rural produce, especially rubber. The urban grocery shops also play a double, or rather a triple, role: they retail goods to urban customers, but they are also the sources from which the rural grocers obtain their stocks, and at the same time, middlemen between rural shops and exporters in the rubber trade. There is thus a sort of two-way traffic in groceries and rubber, and

---

1. Department of Trade & Customs; Annual Statistics 1948. The following figures give a general picture of Sarawak's export trade :-

	1947	1948
Total exports - value in $	103,138,575	171,250,887
Oil products	51,226,596	110,408,494
Agricultural products	51,911,959	60,842,393
(Rubber	26,084,589	34,532,924
(Sago	10,598,863	11,124,325
(Jelutong		
(refined	1,151,076	1,342,650
(raw	1,342,650	885,829
(Pepper		
(white	3,118,384	1,119,935
(black	95,113	39,307
(Copra	50,448	1,040,412
(Vegetable tallow	1,897,428	5,061

2. Such things as biscuits, blachan, candles, dried chillies, coffee, some kinds of crockery, curry stuffs, fireworks and crackers, dried and canned fish, flour, beans, rice, groundnuts, lard, macaroni, margarine, matches, melon-seeds, condensed milk, vegetable oils, onions and garlic, potatoes, salt, sauces, soap, sugar, tea, cotton cloth and yarns, sarongs, handkerchiefs, and some made-up garments, tobacco, toothbrushes and paste, paper umbrellas, fresh and preserved vegetables, vermicelli and vinegar. (This list is also from the above annual report).

it is possible to describe its organisation from either end.

The Chinese in Sarawak themselves divide the different types of rubber middlemen into three grades.[1] The small rural shops which collect rubber from the planters and distribute groceries on credit in return are rubber dealers of the third rank. They do not themselves deal direct with the exporters, but hand their rubber on to the bazaar shops, whose owners are the rubber dealers of the second rank. These second rank dealers act mainly as middlemen between the rural shops and the exporting firms, but some of them also have direct contacts with the planters. The few exporting firms, the first rank, at the top have no direct dealings with either the planters or the rural shops, but only with second rank dealers. The following Table expresses these ascending grades of rubber dealer in diagrammatic form:-

TABLE 14

LADDER OF RUBBER TRANSACTIONS AMONG THE OVERSEAS CHINESE IN SARAWAK

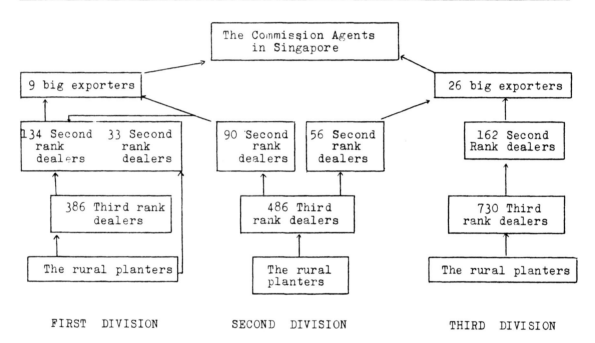

FIRST DIVISION   SECOND DIVISION   THIRD DIVISION

The different grades of rubber dealer may now be analysed according to dialect grouping. Data collected from the records of the Department of Rubber Control and from the Customs Department, together with the results of the writer's own investigations in Kuching and Sibu in 1949 are combined in Table 15.

1. All rubber dealers hold Government licences. For licensing purposes Government divides the dealers into two grades only: exporters and dealers within the Colony. Export licences cost $100, internal rubber dealing licences $5. This classification is not detailed enough for the present study, since it makes no distinction between the small rubber middlemen in the rural areas and the bazaar (urban) middlemen. Moreover it is not always safe to rely upon the figures of registered licence holders: it is not uncommon to find a single shop taking out more than one licence, or a dealer or exporter may not actually make use of a licence once he has taken it out. The figures of registered rubber exporters and dealers are, however, useful in showing the clear predominance of the Chinese in this trade. For example in 1948 in the First Division there were 51 licensed exporters, 46 of them Chinese, and 578 dealers, 524 Chinese. The figures in the Tables attached to this chapter were obtained from my own investigation in 1948.

T A B L E   15

DIALECT   DIFFERENCES   AMONG   THE   RUBBER   DEALERS   OF   DIFFERENT   RANKS

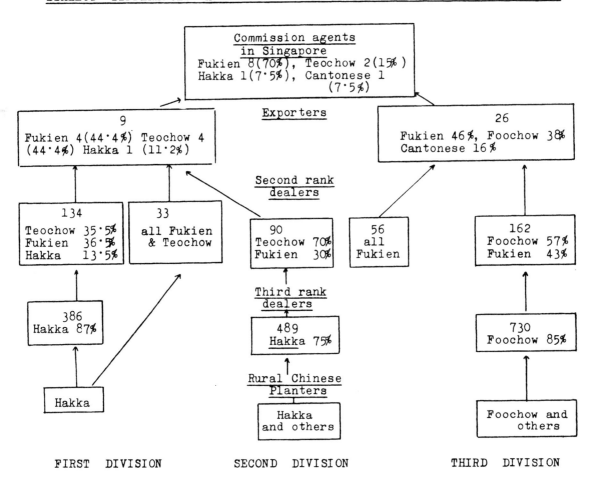

FIRST   DIVISION   SECOND   DIVISION   THIRD   DIVISION

This **Table** shows the whole ladder of rubber dealing relations between the rural planters in Sarawak and the commission agents in Singapore. The predominance of Hakka speaking people among the producers in the First and Second Divisions, and of Foochow speaking people in the same position in the Third Division, which has already been remarked, is paralelled by a similar relative preponderance of these two dialect groups among the third rank dealers. The proportion of Hakkas drops abruptly in the grade of second rank dealer: to 13·5% in the First Division and nil in the Second Division. These second rank dealers, owning shops in the urban bazaars are overwhelmingly Teochows and Fukienese. Even in the Third Division, with its relatively disproportionate number of Foochow people, 43% of the second rank dealers are Fukienese. This does not mean that no Teochow or Fukienese runs a rural shop; some certainly do. But when such a Fukienese shop exists, then very frequently it belongs to the second rank, dealing directly with the exportingfirms, despite its rural location. Very frequently, too, a Teochow or Fukienese shop in a rural area is found to be financially dominant over the whole rural bazaar.

Of the 9 exporters in Kuching 4 are Fukienese, 4 Teochow and 1 Hakka. Certain Second Division dealers of the second rank send their rubber to Kuching; others send their to ports in the Third Division. In the Third Division there are 26 exporters, 12 of whom are Fukienese, 10 Foochow and 4 Cantonese. The dominance of the Fukienese rather than the Foochow people as exporters even in the predominantly Foochow Third Division is well illustrated by the corresponding figures for the sago trade. Sago production is carried on almost entirely by Melanau producers in the Third Division. All the exporters and most of the dealers are Fukienese.[1] This dominance of Teochows and Fukienese (more particularly Fukienese from near Amoy) is further noticeable in Singapore itself.

Thus the division into dialect groups which we have seen above as corresponding with a vertical division into occupational groups, can be viewed to some extent in a different way as corresponding with a horizontal division into economic strata. When each occupation is viewed separately the dialect divisions appear thus :

T A B L E 16

DIALECT AND OCCUPATION.

Clock & watch shops	Tinsmiths	Carpenters	Fishermen	Bicycle shops	Tailors	Coffee etc. shops
CANTONESE	HAKKA	SOUTH MANDARIN	HENGHUA	HENGHUA	HAKKA	HAINAN

But when the whole process of the rubber trade is viewed at once, the dialect lines appear thus:-

T A B L E 17
DIALECT AND ECONOMIC STATUS

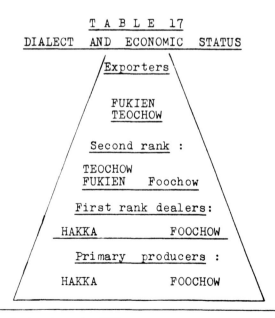

Exporters

FUKIEN
TEOCHOW

Second rank :

TEOCHOW
FUKIEN   Foochow

First rank dealers:

HAKKA   FOOCHOW

Primary producers :

HAKKA   FOOCHOW

1. See note at end of chapter (p.58).

It was suggested above that the vertical lines of occupational identification were tending to give place to horizontal lines between employer and employed. There seems little doubt that this is so. But at the same time the tendency is for certain dialect groups (namely Teochow and Fukien) only to be in the employer class. It is these same groups who are at the top of the commercial pyramid too.

An explanation of this distribution of dialect groups requires an analysis of the structure of economic relations which is undertaken in the following chapter.

Note concerning the Chinese dealers of the Melanau area of the Third Division.

1. There are 5 businesses concerned with the export of sago in Mukah. Three of these are branches of Kuching firms, two are local; all are Fukienese, The Foochow population of Mukah, Oya, Dalat, the principal sago producing districts, is smaller than in any other district of the Third Division but the Fukien (Hokkien) population in these places is relatively large. (See Appendix III).

The distribution of grocery shops also illustrates the same point:-

Mukah : 24 grocery shops   -   9 Teochow,
                                 7 Fukien,
                                 2 Chao An,
                                 1 Cantonese,
                                 5 Foochow (all opened since the war).

Oya   : 19 grocery shops   -   13 Fukien,
                                 3 Teochow,
                                 2 Chao An,
                                 1 Hainan.

Dalat : 34 grocery shops   -   15 Chao An,
                                 5 Fukien,
                                 5 Hainan,
                                 3 Cantonese,
                                 6 Foochow (3 opened since the war).

VIII

BAZAAR ECONOMY AND THE RUBBER TRADE

In discussing clanship we were able to show how the social bonds of genealogical relationship provide the framework of economic activity in the rural districts; in a not very dissimilar way the social bonds of dialect grouping may be described as the framework of the urban economy of Sarawak.

The discussion of the lines of occupational identification in the last chapter gave what might be called a "static" description of the organisation of urban economic activity; a more dynamic presentation may be obtained from a consideration of the machinery of financial relations.

It was suggested in the preceding chapter that in certain trades the development of a class of individuals with enough capital to employ others was tending to bring about the break down of the old lines of occupational identification. At the same time there is a strong tendency for all employers to be members of either the Fukien or Teochow dialect groups. The concentration of capital in the hands of these two groups is clearly recognised by other Chinese in Sarawak. Various Hakka informants complained ruefully that they knew there was no possibility for them to attain financial power or even commercial success. The Teochows and Fukienese, they said, had all the experience of urban life and commercial enterprise, while the rural Hakka had none. Even to the casual observer there seems to be something in this argument: for instance, the Fukienese and Teochow shops are always neatly arranged, the various goods stacked in orderly and pleasing manner; Hakka wares are almost invariably higgledy-piggledy. Similarly, Fukienese and Teochow salesmanship has a skill and finesse of which the Hakka are completely ignorant: a new customer is flattered and cajoled into buying, and his future patronage assured by the offer of specially favourable prices: the Hakka do not bother. Actually Teochow and Fukienese informants also grumbled about the Hakka, pointing out that whereas before the war there were no Hakka shops in Kuching, now there were several such upstarts, and complaining that although the Hakka were too poor to contribute towards its expenses they benefited most from public welfare work. This is, of course, a clear case of success breeding success, but an understanding of this distribution of dialect groups requires a fuller economic analysis.

In Chapter VI we described the organisation of the grocery trade in the rural areas, and stated that its essential complement was the trade in rubber for export. In this chapter we deal with the organisation and finance of this rubber trade. In order to make the general picture as clear as possible, we give first a short description of the ordinary methods of financing such an export trade. Next we go on to investigate the actual organisation of rubber export between Sarawak and Singapore. Then we turn to the question of the internal organisation of the trade within the country, and the ways in which it is involved with the trade in imports and the elaborate structure of credit relationships which we have already touched upon in Chapter VI.

The Financing of the Export Trade

Generally speaking the methods of operation followed by a large exporting firm are something like this: around, say, March the Singapore branch sells on the Singapore market a quantity of rubber for forward delivery in July. The price, of course, is that prevailing in the futures market in Singapore in March. The Kuching agents are then instructed to buy rubber for July delivery in Singapore at not more than such-and-such a price, leaving margins to cover shipping charges, commission and so forth. The Kuching agents thus have about three months in which to buy their rubber for shipment. Once the rubber is actually shipped, the bill of lading, together with the Customs receipt, constitutes a document of title which the shipper can discount at a bank for cash. The banker then posts the bill of lading to his Singapore office, from which the Singapore consignee obtains it by refunding the sum which the Kuching bank advanced to the shipper.

Firms with large capital resources and branches in Singapore can follow this procedure with little risk. Operating on the Singapore rubber market at world prices, they can sell firm for forward delivery and then give their Kuching branches clear instructions as to just what quantities of rubber have to be bought by what date and at what price. The Kuching agents have to have ready cash for their purchases, but a big firm can always borrow from the banks. Generally speaking, the price they have to pay is the spot market price in Kuching, which is normally substantially lower than the spot market price in Singapore. Of course, if the Kuching buyers hold off until the last moment in the expectation that the price will fall, and it does not, they may be caught short. Then, in order to complete the Singapore contract within the specified dates they have to buy rubber in Kuching not only at a price above that of the March forward price, but even above the spot price prevailing in Singapore at the time. A really big firm is not likely to be caught like this, or if it were could afford the risk. The smaller firms, operating on their own, are likely to be in a much more ambiguous position, partly because they have no branches in Singapore, and so must deal with brokers who play the market, and partly because they have not enough capital of their own. They probably find it much more difficult to get a firm forward contract, and they may have to buy rubber in Sarawak simply on the speculation that eventually they will be able to sell it at a profit.

The "Big Nine" in Kuching.

If this analysis is correct we may expect to find that the large exporting firms in Kuching are those whose position is assured both by wealth of capital and by links with Singapore. Lesser firms would be fluctuating all the time, never likely to enter the top ranks unless they too became agents of Singapore firms. Generally speaking that is just the picture we do find. As the following table shows there are only nine or ten Chinese exporters in Kuching whose monthly Customs payments amount to $2,000 or nearly.

TABLE 18

EXPORT DUTY PAID ON LOCAL PRODUCTS - JULY / NOVEMBER 1948 [1]

Exporting Firm	Value in Dollars - 1948	
	July	November
A (Chinese)	53,915	33,022
B "	54,909	16,772
C "	22,755	9,255
D "	18,767	10,184
E "	7,084	2,320
F "	7,271	2,284
G "	-	13,353
H "	1,934	5,116
I "	1,252	-
J " [2]	1,586	-
K (European)	14,081	-
L "	1,739	-
M "	605	-
TOTAL:	183,877	92,106
Percentage of total export duty paid:	55%	75%

It is these firms which have been described in a preceding chapter as "the big exporters", rubber dealers of the first rank. In July 1948, the best month for export in that year, these firms, together with the three European exporters, were responsible for more than half (55%) of the total export from Kuching, the remaining 45% being spread among as many as 51 smaller firms (46 Chinese and 5 Dayak). In November almost every firm exported much less, and the "big nine" accounted for 75% of the total.[3]

The following diagram helps to explain the strength of the "big nine" :-

---

1. Figures obtained from the Department of Trade and Customs, Kuching.

2. Now out of business.

3. In this month even the European exporters dropped out altogether.

T A B L E   19

RELATIONS BETWEEN THE LARGE SCALE CHINESE RUBBER EXPORTERS IN KUCHING
AND THE DEALERS IN SINGAPORE

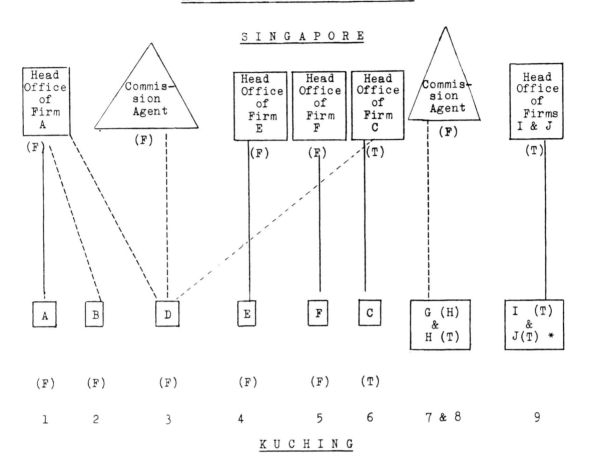

SINGAPORE

KUCHING

F - Fukienese

T - Teochow

H - Hakka

* Now out of business.

There are in all 140 rubber dealers in Singapore; this Table shows that
the "big nine" in Kuching have regular trading arrangements with 7 of them. Five
of the "big nine" are, indeed, really branches of Singapore firms; the other
four act as commission agents. All but one of the big Kuching exporters is
linked with a Singapore firm run by a member of the same dialect group - the
majority being Fukienese, and the rest Teochow.[1] Occupational identification is
thus visible here also. The relationship is often closer than that: for example, the head of the Singapore and Kuching branches of firm A is the same man;
firms B and D in Kuching, who both act as commission agents for A's Singapore

1. The one exception is a Hakka firm in Kuching, whose owner although the son
   of a Hakka was frequently described to the writer as "Not really a Hakka -
   but a Fukienese".

branch both originate from the same Fukien hsien with him; firm C trades with his brother. Once the larger amounts of capital become concentrated in the hands of members of a single dialect group, or still more of a smaller group within that dialect group, they are likely to remain so concentrated. Non-Fukien and non-Teochow firms in Sarawak might therefore be expected to be at a disadvantage.

The Disadvantages of Smaller Firms

The close connections between the big nine in Kuching and their Singapore agents are not only important in that they make it possible for them to deal in futures, there is also the factor of commercial ethics to be considered. Without personal, usually dialect-linked, relationships of mutual trust there is usually no guarantee of fair dealing across such a wide distance. The bigger firms in Kuching have such relations of mutual reliability with their head offices or agents in Singapore. The smaller firms have, as a rule, no such relationships or regular contacts; they are therefore at the mercy of the Singapore firms, and once their rubber has left Kuching they have no more control over it. They simply have to accept whatever price they are given, and the rather rapid fluctuation in price, together with the practice of holding back in order to catch the market, give ample scope for fraud.

This is one of the reasons why the smaller firms are usually more willing to sell to the big Kuching exporters on the spot.

The smaller dealers themselves complain also of the actual expenses of export, declaring that the costs of package, carriage, wharf labour and Customs dues are too heavy for them to bear. Whatever the price of rubber these costs remain fairly constant, amounting to about $8.40 in Kuching and $7.77 in Sibu.[1] The smaller men allege not only that the bigger firms are more able to meet the costs, but also that they are able to cut down expenses through their influence with the shipping companies. The complaint that the larger exporters were always able to secure priority on the boats to Singapore was several times made in my hearing. It is, of course, impossible to prove or

---

1. Details of figures collected from informants in Kuching and Sibu, July 1949.

T A B L E   20

COSTS   PER   PICUL   OF   RUBBER   EXPORTED

KUCHING	$	SIBU	$
Weighing	.80	Cord	.05
Package	.08	Boat transport	2.00
Cord	.10	Wharf labour, Sibu	.55
Lorry transport	.04	" " Singapore	.80
Boat transport	2.00	Insurance	1.00
Wharf labour, Kuching	.21	Deterioration	.22
" " Singapore	1.00	Bank charges	.35
Insurance in warehouse	.03	Export duty (varies each	
" on board ship	.08	month)	3.70
Deterioration	.10		7.77
Commission	.45	For comparison: Costs per dang	
Bank Charges	.26	(133 lbs) sago exported. Sibu.	
Interest	.20		$
Customs duty (varies each		Bag	.95
month)	3.70	Transport	.90
	8.40	(Sibu) Wharf Labour	.40
		Insurance & Bank charges	.20
		Singapore commission *	.40
		Deterioration	.10
		Export duty	1.00
			3.95

* includes payment Singapore labour, etc.

disprove this charge. It is certainly true that a virtual monopoly over ocean going transport is held by a single shipping company and that one of the largest exporters is an important shareholder in this concern.[1]

The smaller firms are at a further disadvantage in that they have no large storage facilities. A large firm is able to buy widely when prices are favourable, and if it has collected too much rubber for its immediate contracts it can store for later shipment, or in addition to its contracts for forward delivery it can engage in speculation with the spot market prices, holding back and waiting for the best opportunity to sell. The smaller men tend to export only when they are perfectly assured of a good price. The difference between the "good" and "bad" months in 1948 shown in Table 16 above, clearly illustrates this tendency.

For these reasons it is not surprising to find that the smaller exporters in Kuching remain as dealers of the second rank. Their direct export trade to Singapore is usually subsidiary to their major businesses of importing grocery and other goods and selling rubber to one or other of the "big nine" in Kuching itself. Usually a second rank dealer is willing to export his own rubber direct only in one or other of the following four circumstances: first he may have a contract with a Singapore firm guaranteeing to buy his rubber at any time at a fixed price. Such a contract is, of course, a gamble for both sides, and both sides stand a more or less equal chance of gain or loss over a period of time. Secondly, a Singapore firm which is badly in need of additional rubber may offer to reduce its commission fee and/or to pay the costs, or a part of the costs, of wharf labour. This is an occasional chance which it may pay the smaller Sarawak firm to seize. In the third place a second-rank dealer in Kuching is, as we shall see, often in need of credit, he may therefore send rubber to Singapore, hoping for a loan from there, or, finally, he may export his rubber direct with the object of raising a loan at home, against the security offered to him by the bill of lading and the Customs receipt.

Rubber export for the smaller firms is thus essentially speculative, and the dealers tend constantly to take a short term view. Speculation by the bigger firms is significant too, but they are in a better position to spread their losses. Generally speaking the aim of the smaller exporter is simply to make as much money as possible out of a single deal, there being no other means of acquiring capital save by the lucky outcome of some such commercial gambles - or by borrowing.

So far, then, we have a picture of the organisation of rubber export between Kuching and Singapore which is largely in the hands of about nine big Chinese firms and three European companies. There are in addition a fluctuating number of smaller firms, second rank dealers, who are mainly concerned with import, but who sometimes export on their own account. The majority of

---

1. The Sarawak Steamship Company, though small in itself, is affiliated through Mansfield & Co., the Singapore Managing agents, with the powerful Straits Steamship Company and effective competition hardly exists.

The Sarawak Steamship Company makes a separate contract with each exporter, the terms of which bind the latter to confine their goods to ships of that company only. Thus other companies cannot get a foothold - except occasionally when a Chinese exporter manages to dodge his contract by signing with another shipping company under an assumed name. In 1947 a group of Chinese was actually operating quite a sizeable steamer on a regular direct run between Sibu and Singapore, but this had closed down by 1949.

the big exporters are Fukienese.[1]

Credit and the Internal Organisation of the Rubber Trade

The structure of the internal organisation of the rubber trade in Sarawak has been summarised in the preceding chapter.[2] The "big nine", as we saw there, have no direct dealings with the rural sellers (third rank dealers) or producers but buy from the second rank dealers, some of whom deal only with third rank dealers, others with rural producers direct as well. The second rank dealers are thus the key middlemen. Now, however the trade is operated between Kuching and Singapore, the Kuching sellers cannot receive any cash proceeds until the rubber is actually loaded on to a ship at Kuching. This means that the rubber must be purchased from the rural rubber dealer or producer either by promissory note or by the payment of actual cash or goods. But the second rank dealers with their limited capital resources have to borrow the cash, or obtain the goods on credit from someone else. So far as cash is concerned that someone else is normally not a bank but one of the "big nine" in Kuching. It is true that a second rank dealer who ships his own rubber to Singapore can get money from a bank as soon as he has a bill of lading, but the purchase of the rubber requires this cash before he comes to shipment. The kind of security which the ordinary second rank dealer can offer to obtain credit of this kind does not satisfy the banks. The wealthy exporters, however, are able and ready to grant loans, and a regular system of borrowing from them against mortgage has come into existence. The security given is usually house property, land (especially rubber holdings) or commercial goods. The term of the loan is usually short, three to six months, with interest at $2\frac{1}{2}\%$ per month. The second rank dealers who sell to Singapore direct speculate in that they must buy rubber from the rural districts without knowing at what price they can sell it. The speculation of those who sell to the big exporters in Kuching is that they can buy at a price sufficiently favourable to make a profit and cover the interest on their loan within the short term allowed.[3]

High interest and short term together give the creditor a strong position. Foreclosure on the mortgage is common. A borrower may ask for an extension of time for payment, but he will only get it at a price. Knowing that he is financially dependent upon the creditor, he finds himself increasingly dependent in other ways too: he may have to sell his rubber a little more cheaply, to promise never to sell it elsewhere, and so forth. At the present time one of the biggest exporters in Kuching has at least eighteen second rank shops fully

---

1. Probably only about half of the big exporters are really secure. The position of the others is itself a matter for speculation. The above description applies to the First and Second Divisions. In the Third Division the major difference, as we have seen, is in the disproportionate number of Foochow people. In Sibu most of the exporters are Foochow. Competition there has reached almost battlefield height, and as a result first one and then another business man finds himself forced out of the game. The list published by the Grocery Association in Sibu* shows that during the three years 1946-9 nearly one third of the grocery shops there have closed down or their owners been declared bankrupt. It is merciless competition, combined with speculation, which explains the spectacular ups and downs of this world of Chinese business. Within 3 months a certain exporter in Kuching made a fortune of $200,000; two months later he was bankrupt, leaving a debt of $50,000 unpaid.**

* Regulations of the Sibu Grocery Association, (in Chinese) 1946.

** Competition on the launch and bus services is also very marked. Official prices per mile are fixed by Government, but all prices actually charged fall below the official figure. In some parts of the Third Division launch journeys are even offered free, with a couple of cigarettes and a meal thrown in. Members of one dialect group often rationalize this situation by complaining bitterly about the members of another, who are obviously incapable of understanding the proper way to make money and whose continual wastefulness nevertheless compels others to reduce their own prices too.

2. See Tables 14 and 15   pp.55 & 56.

3. Loans can be obtained in the same way for every type of purpose.

under his control, while almost all the other second rank dealers are   also
under some greater or lesser obligation to him. Thus the big exporters   are
not only in the best position to control the export trade by reason of their
wealth of capital resources and their connections with Singapore,   they also
command the services of many of the second rank dealers. As the Chinese themselves say of one of them: "he has a finger in every business - except that
of undertaker".

The relationship between second and third rank dealers is also often based
upon credit. Here the second rank dealers are the creditors, but the   credit
offered is less often in money than in goods. In Chapters VI and VII we saw
how in the rural districts the collection of rubber for export and the   distribution of grocery goods from import were both in the hands of the same organisations, the small rural shops, or rubber dealers of the third rank. But
the ladder of export and import trade, so closely linked in the lower rungs, is
divided at the top. It is true that four of the "big nine" in Kuching are also concerned with the import of groceries and other goods, but the biggest of
all are exporters only, and in any case nearly all the second rank   rubber
dealers who are also grocery dealers import their own stock direct from Singapore. Thus the second rank dealers who are usually middlemen between   the
rural shops and the Kuching exporters in the rubber trade, are middlemen between the rural shops and Singapore in the grocery business.

Rubber Collection and Credit Relationships

In the rural districts the rural shops are the centres from which   the
Chinese producers obtain their provisions on credit, and to which   they bring
their rubber. The general shortage of capital makes it imperative for   the
rural shops themselves to get credit from the bazaar shops (second rank dealers) in very similar ways. This is by no means always easy, but the   rural
shops usually manage to get what they want by a process of accumulating debt,
or by agreeing to act as a sort of agent in the rubber trade, or by a combination of the two.

Debt accumulation works as follows: a small outstanding sum of,   say,
about $20 starts the ball rolling; once the small rural shop owner   can get
even this much credit he is well on the way to forcing his creditor to   give
him almost unlimited credit in the future, under the generally accepted   recognition that the full debt never will be paid off unless further credit is
forthcoming. For instance, on opening a new relationship with a shop of the
second rank a rural shop-owner will be very careful to pay the first two or
three accounts promptly and in full. In this way he establishes his reputa-
tion, and then, later, he may ask for, say, 5% or 10% allowance on his   next
account, giving the excuse that he just happens to be short of money for the
time being. Of course the bazaar shop-keeper understands what is happening,
but he has his own interest to consider as well, and he knows that unless he
grants credit in this way he will be able to do no business at all - and, in
any case, he has probably acquired almost all his own stock of goods from Singapore in a similar way. Once the debt has been started in this courteous manner, the debtor will probably try to increase the amount advanced to him each
time - say to 20% or 30% of the total account. The more unscrupulous debtors
may go so far as to demand a full 100%. The creditor knows that if he refuses
he will lose the debt already outstanding, for his customer will transfer his
business elsewhere. Payment or part payment of an outstanding debt is thus by
convention the accepted method of acquiring fresh credit.[1]

1. The working of this system, which applies at every economic level, is well
understood by the people themselves. One of the Chinese Towkays expressed
his view, gained after many years experience, that the secret of doing good
business was not to make a high profit out of one's customers, but to   get
other people's money as capital, since only in this way was it possible   to
build up a large scale business. There is also a saying which may be translated: "Buy for ten, sell for seven, give back three, keep four". This refers with some exaggeration, to a custom which at first sight appears singu-
larly uneconomical. Having bought an article on credit for $10 a man   may
sell it to his customer for $7 and then pay $3 of this back to his creditor.
He then has $4 in his pocket - an effective way of doing business   without
money, and a vivid illustration of the importance of actual cash in a system
where so much of the finance structure consists of debts.

A credit relationship of this type is often connected with an agreement by the debtor to send in his rubber to the creditor. Sometimes the owner of a bazaar shop who is a second rank dealer may be willing to lend money to a rural shopkeeper on condition that the latter act as a rubber collector for him. A bazaar shop owner will probably only do this if he is personally assured, usually through some form of personal contact, of the other's reliability.

Ex-employees who have set up on their own as small rural shopkeepers are often treated in this way - almost as small branch stores; surname relationships also act as a personal bond for this purpose, the difference between this clan tie and that within the rural areas themselves being that this is not localised, while it depends also upon factors of personality and familiarity; there is also the network of close kinship ties, brother trusting the integrity of brother, for example. The rural shopkeeper who receives money in this way can then use it to extend his own business, or to lend to others, or buy land or a pig or whatnot, and periodically he sends in the rubber he has collected to his creditor in Kuching. This kind of loan is granted without interest, and stands so long as the rural shopkeeper continues to send in rubber. When the price of rubber is favourable to the Kuching shops (i.e. when it is low) then the rural shops will be asked to settle their accounts for the preceding period.

These, in fact, are the most economical methods of rubber collecting for the second rank dealers to adopt. And they are usual ones. They avoid the expenses which would be necessary for the setting up of special branches in the rural areas or the employment of special agents on commission or salary. In effect the rural shops with arrangements such as those just outlined act as agents to the second ranks with whom they are connected. Such arrangements are the most satisfactory for both sides. They are usually long term relationships, built up upon mutual trust depending upon personal contacts.[1] A rural dealer or producer who urgently requires money without such a long term relationship will take his rubber to Kuching himself and try to sell it to the highest bidder. But not many second rank dealers are willing to buy in this way, and a rural dealer or producer who relied upon this alone would find he had made a mistake in the long run. He would have no regular established relationships.

The actual day to day organisation of rubber collecting (and grocery distribution) in Sarawak is closely affected by the peculiar system of communications. This, in Sarawak is mainly water-borne, carried in launches of which there are on the registered lists of the Shipping Department, 112 (ranging from 4 to 56 tons), centred in Sibu, and 76 (6 to 224 tons) centred in Kuching. There are many small unregistered launches, especially in the First Division. The bigger Chinese owned launches belong either to the richer firms, such as the big exporters, the larger second-rank-dealers-cum-grocery-stores, and large scale contractors, or to a group of smaller shop-owners from a bazaar, for example in Bintulu or Mukah, who have clubbed together to buy a boat which they then use for transporting their own goods and, usually, also as a public vehicle. The larger firms, who control their own internal communications in this way are able to collect rubber when and where they will, and can cut down on transport expenses while at the same time making a profit out of the fees charged to others. For the second rank dealers who, as we have seen, are speculating that the rubber they buy can be sold at a profit, this control of water transport may well be crucial. Some of the smaller firms too, possess their own launches, or have a share in a jointly held boat, and they too stand to gain once the initial outlay has been covered. (A small launch - 4-6 tons - cost about $4,000 in 1949). Others have to rely upon launches which are run for the profit either by the bigger firms already mentioned, or by private individuals, or by such bodies as certain Chinese school boards which have bought a launch with money raised by public subscription with the object of devoting the profits its brings in to the benefit of their school. Very similar general

---

1. This explains one of the disadvantages of the European firms in Sarawak. Because they have no personal contacts in the rural bazaars they are not in a position to grant advances in this way.

considerations apply to the organisation of bus transport in Sarawak, where it exists.

In the First Division arrangements between rural dealers and Kuching shops very, sometimes one and sometimes the other paying the transport fees. As a general rule launch owners do not act as commission agents. In the Second and Third Divisions, owing to the greater distance, arrangements are different. In the Second Division many of the launch owners actually buy the rubber from the rural dealers. The launch owners are thus themselves second rank dealers, or, rather, the launches are used by second rank dealers as their method of buying - either because they own the launches and employ the drivers, or because the drivers act as commission agents. The biggest exporters also own launches which go to the Third Division to collect sago, and also rubber,from bazaar centres such as Mukah. In the First Division there is such a continual coming and going of small craft that it is not worth a big dealer's while to organise his own collecting arrangements.

The internal distribution of grocery goods is, of course, also mainly by launch. Rural shops can send in lists of their requirements, together with cash, in payment or part payment, or rubber on account. Transport expenses are settled either by the buyer or the seller according to their private arrangement. Usually, as we have seen, the relationship between rural shops and Kuching shops is a long-standing one. Sometimes, however, a launch driver may be given a list of goods which cannot be supplied by the usual shop, or the rural shopkeeper may wish to engage in some "back door" transaction. In such cases the launch driver may act as rather more than a mere transport agent.

Grocery Import and its Control

The method of dealing between the Sarawak retailers and the wholesale firms in Singapore is simple. By every boat the latter send lists of available goods and current prices from which the Sarawak firms make their orders by post. Transport is paid by the buyer. It is not easy to arrange for an advance from a Singapore firm, but an arrangement to delay payment until the next boat comes in, or later, is not uncommon.

Now just as command of export is largely in the hands of Fukienese, so command of the import of grocery goods may be described as a Teochow speciality. In terms of occupational grouping we have already discussed this Teochow identification in the preceding chapter. The following diagram shows the dialect distribution of grocery stores in Sarawak and their links with the Singapore firms. Comparison with Tables 14 & 15 above shows the close relationship between the ladders of import and export which have already been stressed.

T A B L E   21

IMPORT RELATIONSHIPS BETWEEN FIRST DIVISION SARAWAK AND SINGAPORE.[1]

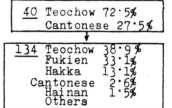

A. Singapore wholesale merchants	40 Teochow 72·5% Cantonese 27·5%
B. Bazaar retailers (Kuching)	134 Teochow 38·9% Fukien 33·1% Hakka 13·1% Cantonese 2·6% Hainan 1·5% Others
C. Rural retailers (First Division)	438 Hakka 79% Teochow 14% Fukien 5% Cantonese 2%

1. Figures for the rural retailers are only approximations, as the writer was unable to visit every rural bazaar personally. The Kuching figures were collected by personal observation (1948-9), and those for Singapore are taken from <u>Post war Commerce and Industry in Singapore</u> (in Chinese) by Hsu Yun-Tsao and Hsu Chih 1948. Hainanese coffee shops are omitted.

The large number of Hakka shops in the rural districts we have already described as being due to the large preponderance of Hakka in the peasant population. In Kuching, however, the Hakka drop back to third place, and among the Singapore wholesale merchants not one is to be found. Even in the rural districts of the First Division quite a large number of the grocery stores are Teochow, while in Kuching and, more especially, in Singapore Teochows are completely dominant. The Cantonese and Teochow position in Singapore may be said to be largely due to the fact that the Chinese groceries they deal in come mainly from the vicinity of Canton and Swatow; the Teochow group has a particular advantage in the rice trade, most of which comes from Siam where the Chinese population is almost exclusively Teochow.1 The position of the Fukienese illustrates from a different angle the division between the channels of import and export which occurs at the higher levels. Fukienese number very nearly as many as Teochow grocery shops in Kuching, but not in Singapore, since Fukien province is not a source of Chinese grocery goods. Yet we have seen how the Fukienese grocer shops in Sarawak are linked by their rubber trade with the Fukienese firms in Singapore who dominate the export market. Thus the division between export and import trading channels is to be seen not simply as a concomitant of the greater ease and security for the export trade offered by the development of large scale exporting business in Kuching, but also as connected with the Teochow (and to a lesser extent Cantonese) advantage in the import trade. The economic division tends, once more, to be also a dialect division, and once again we can see that social relationships provide the channels for economic activity while at the same time economic relationships recreate and fortify the solidarity of social groupings.

In this chapter I have tried to show that the present system of financing the rubber export trade from Sarawak calls for a small number of entrepreneur capitalists of substantial resources. As there is only room for a very limited number of such capitalists, it is not surprising to find the major part of the trade concentrated in the hands of half a dozen or so Fukien firms. Teochow firms also play some part in this export trade, but are mainly concerned with the import trade in the most important type of which (in grocer's goods) they are completely dominant. Since the export of rubber and the import of grocer's goods, which might be called reciprocal processes, are the mainstay of the Chinese economy in Sarawak, the groups which dominate in these two businesses are likely to dominate the Chinese community as a whole. In the next chapter we shall see how far it is true that the powerful members of the Fukien and Teochow groups are also the leaders of the Chinese community.

IX

T H E   P R O B L E M   O F   P O W E R

The foregoing analysis of the economic conditions of bazaar and rural areas has shown the economic strata in the Chinese community arranged like a pyramid. At the bottom there is the huge majority of Chinese planters and labourers, the workers by whose sweat and lives primary jungle has been transformed into cultivated land; in the middle there is the fairly numerous class of small and smallish merchants, the middlemen who gather in local products and hand out imported goods, maintaining the fluidity of the economic system by dealing with the rural workers on the one hand and the big merchants and foreign companies in Kuching on the other; at the top are the few big towkays. It is the members of this top class who are usually termed "leaders" and looked upon as representatives of the overseas Chinese as a whole. Their actual

1. At the time of writing the import of rice (and sugar) is subject to government control, and the grocery firms are rationed.

relationship with members of the two other main classes of Chinese, and the small group of professional people, is the subject of this chapter.[1]

Ever since the beginning of Brooke rule in the 1840's, the "administration" of the Chinese community, that is the control of it by the Colonial Government, has been effected broadly speaking by the principle that has of late come to be known as "indirect rule". That is, the British authorities have selected from the local Chinese community persons who appeared to have the greatest influence and appointed them as official "leaders" of the Chinese, traditionally with the Dutch title of Kapitan China, but nowadays sometimes with other titles. Apart from this, interference with the internal administration of the Chinese community by the paramount authority has been minimal. The tendency rather has been to treat "the Chinese" as a single entity; contact between the Administration and "the Chinese" has then been maintained exclusively through the channel of "recognised Chinese Leaders". This policy has in general been justified by the argument that no European could reasonably be expected to understand the complexities of Chinese society, and provided the authorities intervened occasionally to prevent manifest abuse, the less it interfered the better. As others have phrased it, the Chinese community in each of the South East Asian territories is treated as "a State within a State". In this chapter however I shall bring forward facts which suggest that this policy of non-intervention does not really operate in the manner that the authorities presumably intend. The whole body of this book has served to emphasise that to treat "the Chinese" as a single political entity is a gross oversimplification. The main emphasis of the present chapter is to show that those whom the Administration approves as "recognised Chinese leaders" are not in fact, in any democratic sense, representative of the community whose interests they are supposed to serve.

As things are at present, economic strength is the path to social power. In other words wealth and political privilege go hand in hand. A financially powerful towkay automatically gains a high social position, and social position, together with political privilege, in turn brings increased wealth. The circle is complete. Nearly all the so-called Chinese "leaders" are wealthy men.[2] Therefore in discussing the relationships between the rich towkays at the top of the economic pyramid and the rest, we are discussing the problems of social power within the Chinese community.

It therefore goes without saying that the most influential dialect groups in the First Division are the Fukienese and the Teochows. The actual numerical preponderance of the Hakkas goes for nothing. The power of the Fukienese lies in their financial strength, of the Teochows in the number of their business units. As leaders of the community they are continual rivals, but the division of economic roles means that in fact one can do nothing without the other. Thus whereas the Chairman of the Chamber of Commerce is a Fukienese, the vice-chairman is a Teochow. The fact that the Fukienese Chairman is usually absent appears to leave the field to the Teochows, but actually Fukienese supporters continue to pull strings behind the scenes. The Teochow group no matter how numerous their business units, depend to some extent upon Fukienese for the supply of capital. Thus the balance of social power between the two groups is continually self-adjusting.

Patronage.

This social power is highly concentrated. As we shall see, social conditions in Sarawak are such that a few individuals are able to make their influence penetrate into almost every aspect of social life, thus bringing the general Chinese public almost completely under their control. No one in the Chinese community can advance without a "back mountain", as it is called. In other words, a highly developed system of patronage exists. Teacher, business

---

1. It is, of course, somewhat unfair to discuss the position of the Chinese towkays without dealing with the whole economic system within which they carry on their business. There have been a number of studies of Colonial economics in South East Asia, however, and since my work has been deliberately limited to the boundaries of the Chinese community itself I am concentrating here upon the internal relationships between those Chinese who are at the top of the social-economic ladder and the rest.
2. A few are not, see below.

man, coolie - all depend on patronage, and the size of a patron's "clientele" is thus an index of his social power. The most powerful men whose influence is fully established are not easily approachable, but the efforts of smaller men to build up their own following can be observed freely, and from them it is possible to discuss the process by which social power is acquired. Basically it is compounded of economic strength and official recognition.

Broadly speaking the process of acquiring social power is the same in both town and country. As we have seen the economic organisation of the First Division of Sarawak is welded together by systems of credits and loans. Because it is not profitable to lend money to the small rural shops, financial control as such is directly exercised only between the big financiers (exporters and money-lenders in Kuching) and the rubber dealers of the second rank. We have already pointed out that characteristic features of business in Sarawak are the lack of capital and the emphasis upon speculation: both of which provide ideal conditions for those who lend money to extend their influence. Thus in Sarawak, as in all the Chinese communities of the Nan Yang, one constantly hears the word "back-mountain". It comes like a kind of refrain:"One cannot do business without a strong back-mountain", "Old so-and-so is very lucky to have Mr. X as his back-mountain", and so forth. Thus, the chief "back-mountains" are those who can lend money on a large scale.But money lending involves risks. At the present time there are two main types of large scale money lender in Kuching; one is willing to take risks, and not averse to helping his debtors with further advances, the other risks as little as possible, squeezing the last penny from the empty purse. Those of the first type may or may not prosper, at least they are more popular;[1] the second type go steadily on collecting their interest and consolidating their financial position. Smaller money lenders are also very numerous.

Since it is the accepted rule that "If you use my money you must obey my order", financial relationships are closely involved with other, apparently unrelated, social obligations. Thus although by no means all the holders of social power in the Chinese community are lenders of money, yet it is more usual to find social power built upon financial strength.

Election to Office:

This wide-spread system of patronage makes the normal routine for the election of representatives wholly ineffective. Association officials hold office for only one year, after which they must stand for re-election by allegedly secret ballot. It is notorious that in some Chinese Associations, the same officials are returned year after year. Why is this? The usual listed membership of an Association is about two or three hundred poeple, but only about thirty to sixty bother to vote. Members who are not attached to the chairman by bonds of debt are not bound to please him and so need not trouble themselves; those who are so bound cannot vote otherwise than for their creditor. Any debtor who goes to the poll knows for whom he must vote. All this does not apply to Associations whose chairmen are not of the richest and most influential class, but it is certainly widely believed that in some Associations not only is the ballot not secret but the chairman often actually checks over the voting papers in order to decide which of his debtors should be favoured with a further loan and which dunned for repayment.[2]

Such manipulation of Association elections may not appear very serious, much the same might be said of the election of Directors at British Company meetings, or the election of office bearers at sundry English clubs and learned

---

1. An example of this comparative leniency was a topic of common gossip in Sibu: a certain big firm was said to have paid about $200,000 simply as interest to its creditor, a sum large enough to force the closing of its Sibu branch. At the same time, however, the same firm's Kuching branch still had a large outstanding debt, also about $200,000, to the same financier, and this was not called in.
2. The purely social concomitants of financial obligations are often illustrated in the local press. Paragraphs of congratulations to wealthy Towkays on intimate personal occasions, such as, for instance, the birth of a grandson, are inserted by many of his debtors - sometimes from far distant and most unexpected sources.

Institutions, but it becomes serious when the influence of patronage is extended to the election of those who shall hold political office. For example: As has been shown the bulk of the rural Chinese population in the Sarawak First Division is Hakka. So far as Government is concerned these Hakka are administered through sundry local Capitans China. In the past these Capitans were appointed by the British authorities; the office is now elective. There have recently been four new appointments of Capitans China in this area, based on the electoral choice of an almost exclusively Hakka electorate. On the face of it is surprising that three of these elected representatives of Hakka voters should not be Hakkas! Instead they are business men of the Fukien and Teochow dialect groups belonging to the category of "second class business men" described above. The explanation of this paradox is that the Hakka voters feel the need to keep in the good books of economically powerful patrons of this kind. But having a Fukien Capitan administering a Hakka area does not necessarily lead to good administration.[1]

Government Favour and Official Leadership

The eventual consolidation of one's social power comes when one succeeds in obtaining recognition from the authorities. If one becomes known to administrative officials by other means, then obviously it is not necessary to go through the laborious process of building up a following by financial control. As we shall see there are some wealthy Chinese who prefer to exercise their power behind the scenes, but for those who desire public recognition (and they are the majority) some official position, or at least official approbation, brings at least two advantages: on the one hand, one can occasionally get some favour from Government, on the other hand one can impress the community with one's official "standing", with the result that no smaller fry will dare to offer opposition or offence. Indeed once one has even caught the eye of a European official one's position in the community is automatically strengthened. A socially ambitious Chinese who has been asked to drop in to tea with a European official is likely to boast later that he was entertained to a most luxurious dinner; even a nodding acquaintanceship is magnified for public consumption into a confidential friendship.[2] Again, it would be unfair to generalise thus about every leading Chinese, but nearly all the really powerful gentlemen have travelled at least a part of this way.

Moreover the authorities are usually willing to meet them half-way. There is an understandable eagerness on the part of Government officials to find people willing to act as intermediaries between themselves and the local Chinese. Once having found such people, and noting the way they have built up personal followings, Government also believes that they must have some strong influence of their own - as indeed they have. Influential people must be won for Government co-operation, and this can be done by the granting of occasional small favours. The mass of the local Chinese, impressed with the halo of officialdom, shows great respect to a recognised "leader".

In theory, in Sarawak, direct approach to Government authorities is always possible, but the ordinary Chinese feels that the 'proper channels' of a bureaucratic system are too alarming and the behaviour of officials too unpredictable. For the majority therefore, good relations with the Government appear to depend upon the good offices of the officially recognised "leaders". Thus fearing possibly deliberate misrepresentation, they are careful to show sufficient respect. There is no doubt that certain powerful Chinese do their best to take advantage of this state of affairs, and, though few meet with full success, some have certainly built very snug positions for themselves vis-a-vis both Government and people.

---

1. It is not intended to suggest that the elections are actually tampered with On the contrary the Administration is at pains to make them as secret and democratic as possible.

2. The conspicuous display of titles appears visibly in the use of visiting cards on which all possible official positions of the owner are printed. One leading Chinese in Kuching makes a point of having his secretary write in an additional title, which has been "forgotten", in the presence of guests he wishes to impress.

As I have already said: the whole process is circular. Unto him who hath, much is given. It may be remarked that the fact that so many of the Chinese intermediaries between the authorities and the Chinese community owe their position to the somewhat disreputable system which we have here labelled "patronage", has a generally detrimental effect upon relations between the Administration and the Chinese community as a whole. The ordinary Chinese knows that finance plays an important part in the appointment of his own leaders. He naturally suspects that similar shady relations operate as between these leaders and their European opposite numbers. There is not, so far as I know, the slightest basis for any of these suspicions but it does seem relevant to mention here that all sorts of scandalous talk does circulate among the overseas Chinese concerning the way in which so-and-so got this and so-and-so got that out of the favour and compliance of Government officials.

The Role of the Schools:

Recently the struggle for social power has entered the field of education. As with administration, Government intervention in Chinese schooling has been indirect. Certain grants-in-aid are given, but these do not cover more than a fraction of the total school expenses. Although post-war Government policy is to exercise greater overall control through the Department of Education and the Department of Chinese affairs, the fact is that the Chinese community still to a very large extent finances the education of Chinese children and consequently the location of schools and the appointment of teaching staff tends to be in the hands of the financial leaders of the Chinese community. The enthusiasm for education which all overseas Chinese communities show is not difficult to understand. In China the immigrants or their forefathers experienced the full rigidity of the old Chinese social system, suffering not only from poverty but also from the social distance existing between the privileged and unprivileged classes, for privilege in China did not depend upon wealth alone – indeed however rich he may have been a merchant was always near the bottom of the traditional social scale.[1] At the top stood the officials and the intelligentsia, the peculiar difficulties of the Chinese literary language and the strict system of examinations making the two almost synonymous. In order to build up any sort of prestige a successful merchant had either to establish some kind of kinship relation, affinal or fictitious, with the intelligentsia, or else try to educate his own children. At the same time the prestige value of education was enhanced by the strongly developed 'mystique' of the educated man and of the intrinsic worth of Chinese culture. In the Nan Yang this traditional reverence for education is further reinforced.[2] The number of Chinese who can gain official status in the Colonial administration, or who can come to be regarded officially as "leading personalities" is necessarily few. English education or wealth are the keys to this kind of position. Wealth is inevitably limited to the few, but in theory at least there is sufficient social mobility to make hope for personal advancement spring eternal. Every coolie who comes to the Nan Yang comes to seek his fortune. His own disappointments are comforted if his children can be set upon the way, and, although it is true that by no means all the most powerful Chinese in Sarawak to-day are educated men, yet acquaintance with letters and calculation is undoubtedly generally, and rightly, regarded as an essential first step to prosperity in the modern world.

The Chinese in Sarawak have been opening schools all over the place. Wherever there is a Chinese settlement, however small, there must be a Chinese school. These schools are built and maintained by fees and private subscriptions, and managed by spontaneously organised local school boards. When the general standard of living in some of the rural areas is taken into consideration one can have nothing but the highest admiration for the sacrifice and effort that has gone into the building of some of these schools. I have come across a rural Chinese who, as a member of his local school board, had con-

---

1. The traditional order was: (1) Scholar, (2) farmer, (3) labourer, (4) merchant.

2. Private Chinese schools were run by the old Kongsi Republics in Dutch Borneo, and in the Bau area too, long before there was any European sponsored education.

tributed more than $300 a year, while he himself lived in an atap hut and his family had denied themselves even a single chair or table. In some families school fees take up as much as one-fifth of the whole income, yet parents remain enthusiastic, eager to send their children to school because they still hope for their future.

Let us return to the subject of social power. These schools are being set up for Chinese, on Chinese initiative through Chinese private subscription. This means that wealthy Chinese have a new field to exploit. Some are entirely sincere, moved to contribute their money by a genuine desire to serve the Chinese community, and sharing the prevailing Chinese belief in education whose origins we have just discussed. Others are attracted by the new possibilities of extending their personal influence. In the rural areas the increase in the number of school boards is gradually producing a new type of social organisation, cutting across the old kinship alignments and giving opportunities for the development of a new type of social power. This we shall deal with below. In Kuching all the Chinese schools come under the control of a single board. This comprises about thirty members, including nearly all who can be described as socially powerful. Membership of the educational board sets the seal upon their social power. In China, with a few exceptions, teachers have held a significant social position, with a voice in everything concerning public welfare. Overseas, on the contrary, teachers are socially impotent. The Chinese school board pays, appoints and dismisses all the Chinese teachers in Kuching. But the Chinese school board is composed of the same Chinese who are financially and socially powerful in most other aspects of Chinese community life. The only possible opposition to them could come from the teachers. Thus by their control of the teachers the position of the present holders of power becomes virtually unassailable.

The Monopoly of Leadership:

This brief description of the processes by which social power can be gained and consolidated should not be taken to imply that every leading Chinese in Sarawak is of the same type. On the contrary it is possible to distinguish at least eight different categories. There are, first of all, the really wealthy gentlemen whose power is openly exercised and universally recognised, whose domicile is not necessarily continuously in the Colony and who are ably supported by efficient younger followers; second, there are those, perhaps equally or even more wealthy, who are not interested in social power as such, but only in so far as it brings ever increased riches; third come the also wealthy and also powerful manipulators of power, those who do not desire publicity, but who nevertheless exercise considerable influence behind the scenes; fourth may be listed the European educated, who owe their status less to wealth than to their adaptability to European culture which gives them easy social access to European officials, for example on the tennis courts or at the races, as well as in business or official life; fifth, there are the few influential professional men, not wealthy, not Europeanised, but powerful through their professional shrewdness: successful newspaper editors, leading teachers who are "in with" the educational board. In the sixth category may be counted, unfortunately on the fingers of one hand, the really public spirited personalities who alone deserve the name "leader", not for their wealth, which is often rapidly decreasing, but for their active, disinterested service to the community. All the above six types belong to the towns. In separate seventh and eighth categories may be placed the rural "leaders", first the wealthy and openly powerful, like smaller editions of the first type listed above, and second a new type, often poor, genuinely ready to sacrifice himself in the public educational service. All told, the powerful people in Kuching in all these categories probably number less than forty. In each rural district there may be one or two.

Not all the people we are discussing hold recognised posts, sponsored by the Colonial Government or otherwise. Nearly all of the Kuching "leaders" are members of the Chamber of Commerce or the Educational Board, some are Chairmen of recognised Associations, or hold official appointments such as Capitan China. Most appear in several such positions. In the rural districts they may also be Capitans China or chairmen of the local school boards. Whether in public office or not, however, there is no doubt that these few men have the complete monopoly of control over the public affairs of the entire Chinese community. And every Chinese knows it. Community welfare requires money: only the wealthy "leaders" can supply it. The ordinary people can make suggestions, of course, but they cannot make final decisions because they do not control the purse strings. This public impotence can be documented by example after example. At one Association meeting a young Chinese made an impassioned speech concerning the welfare of the Association members. The chairman, a wealthy towkay, grew impatient. Suddenly he interrupted the young speaker: "How many rubber estates do you own?" The young man answered none. "In that case" said the Chairman, with a sigh, "since you will have nothing to contribute when the subscription list comes round, you had better cut your speech short".

In education this power of wealth is particularly pronounced.The Chinese schools in Kuching to-day are dominated by a system of competitive cramming. The members of the educational board consider that the only aim of education is to pass examinations, and that it is absolutely essential for this purpose to set up prizes for which all the schools can compete. As a result brilliant pupils are crammed beyond endurance, and the others are neglected. Only the traditional academic subjects[1] are taught, and only too often modern methods and out of school activities are ignored. A projected camping expedition in 1949 was summarily forbidden. Many of the teachers deplore the present policy, but there is no point in protesting for the educational board merely replies: "We patronise the school, it is for us to decide". Members have even been heard to complain that of course they cannot be expected just to give away their money, if the teachers want to practise their own schemes then they must be prepared to provide the funds. It is scarcely surprising that the ordinary Chinese sometimes appear apathetic in matters of public concern.

The power holders of Kuching have a remote control over the rural districts as well. This is maintained in two ways: economic and political. The intermeshing of bazaar and rural economies has already been discussed. Both are in the last resort dependent upon the big towkays, but the rural areas being the further removed are the more dependent. In other words, if the ordinary townsman has power only to make a few probably unheeded suggestions,the ordinary countryman has no voice at all in public affairs. As a result the interests of the rural Chinese are largely neglected. All that the rural people can do is to receive instructions from the bazaar "leaders" and carry them out. They contribute money, they send representatives to public meetings - but we have seen what happens at public meetings. It is a significant fact that whereas the most numerous dialect group in the First (and Second) Division is the Hakka group, yet not a single important elective or so-called "representative" post has ever been held by a Hakka speaking person.[2] Hakkas, as we have seen, are mainly rural farmers. The Chinese Chamber of Commerce in Kuching is usually assumed to represent the interests of the whole Chinese community. We have shown that it actually covers only a very small section of even the Kuching Chinese: still less does it represent the rural people.[3]

---

1. Chinese education in Sarawak is not still confined to the Confucian classics, nevertheless the subjects taught and the textbooks used both in Sarawak and elsewhere in the Nan Yang are for the most part deplorably old-fashioned.

2. It is true, of course, that Chinese are equally eligible with the natives of Sarawak to take part in the administration of the country, and do indeed play an important part in paid Government service. In all, five Chinese have been promoted to the Senior Service, and of these three are Hakkas. Both the principal Asian Officers in the Secretariat for Chinese Affairs for the last twenty years have also been Hakkas. But it is well known that the position of the Civil servant is a special one, making him in an important sense politically impotent.

3. It has been objected to the writer that the Chinese Chamber of Commerce in Kuching is not in fact assumed to represent the interests of the Chinese community as a whole, and that it was for this very reason that Chinese Advisory Boards were established after the Japanese War. These boards are attended by the chairmen of all important dialect Associations.Their meetings are not regular, and their functions are, as their name implies, purely advisory.

The Capitan China and Rural Administration :

Politically the control of the big towkays over the rural areas appears to be on the increase. A Chinese rural district comes under the official authority, subject of course to the British administrative officers, of a "Capitan China". In the old days the selected Capitans were nearly always the outstandingly wealthy men of their districts. The system of appointing wealthy Chinese to be the official leaders of their communities was first adopted by the Dutch, and de Groot's work on the Chinese gold-mining companies in West Borneo[1] suggests that they were originally also the "natural leaders" selected by the people themselves. The difficulties of the Chinese languages, and the conspicuous distinctions of Chinese custom made it essential that some method of appointing intermediaries between European Administration and Chinese community should be devised. The Capitan China system, like other systems of Indirect Rule, also proved an easy and economical method of maintaining law and order. It was, and is, not confined to the rural districts, but it is there that it remains most effective to-day. Now in the rural districts wealth is mainly judged by acreage owned. Most of the old Capitans were land-owners, who although often incompetent administrators had at least enough economic independence to act as a check upon arbitrary exactions from any side. Although some had financial relationships with the big towkays none was completely subservient. Some, if not all, owed their position also to descent. There is a certain Capitan China near Bau to-day who claims that he is the fifth of his line, that all his forbears were Capitans China, and that his family was settled in Sarawak before the arrival of the first Rajah. Criticism of the old type of Capitan must be directed to them as individuals: if they were incompetent or unscrupulous they were themselves to blame. Recently, however, a different type of Capitan has been emerging. In the newly opened areas, where jungle is only just being replaced by cultivated land, there has not yet been time for the development of big estates or families of long standing. The post of Capitan in these areas, as elsewhere, still falls to the most influential individuals, but influence here belongs not to independent land holders but to those who have a satisfactory "back mountain", a rich financier, in the background. In the opinion of the ordinary people, too, it is usually felt that a person who has some sort of connection, by kinship or otherwise, with the powerful "leaders" in Kuching is likely to be a more useful Capital than one who has no such ties. They therefore vote for such a one. At any rate all the newly appointed Capitans are so connected.

Somewhere in the First Division four new Capitans China have recently been appointed. Three of these have kinship relations with one of the most influential towkays in Kuching, and the fourth is a personal friend of this same man. It is also worth noting that although the Chinese inhabitants of these districts are almost exclusively Hakka speaking, three of the four new Capitans belong to another dialect group. We have already noted the extension of Towkay power that this implies.[2] It is, to say the least, debatable that the interests of Hakka speaking people can in the present state of Chinese society in Sarawak, be represented by a person from another dialect, but a second result is even worse for the unfortunate Hakkas. In Chapter VI we described their lowly economic status. Most are farmers, the few who are able to set up in business remain limited to small scale enterprises because of the competition of Fukienese and Teochows. Now the three non-Hakka capitans mentioned here are all business men, belonging to the second rank as described in that chapter. That is, they are all economically superior to any local Hakka business men, with greater financial resources and wider business connections. By becoming Capitans China these three men wield a combined political and economic power which, under the present system, can scarcely be controlled. Even the social prestige of office, let alone the actual power,

---

1. J.J.M. de Groot Het Kongsiwesen van Borneo (1885).

2. This is no officially sanctioned relationship, of course. The Chinese in rural districts are not systematically subordinated to the Capitan China in Kuching. There is, in other words, no official hierarchy for the Chinese community as a whole. In official theory each Capitan China is subordinate immediately only to the local British administrative officer.

inevitably has a great effect upon business in these Chinese communities. The rural Hakkas are handicapped in every way.

Originally the Capitan China system may have had considerable practical value, but like other systems of Indirect Rule in other British Colonies it fails to meet modern requirements. Wealth is not necessarily a sign of the qualities desirable in a leader, but simply an index of its owner's go-getting prowess. Neither the Capitans China nor the other holders of public positions, the Chairman and members of the Chamber of Commerce or the educational boards, the Chairman of the dialect and trade associations, are, generally speaking, individuals who would have been chosen if election were by free, secret ballot on a broadly based franchise. They are, instead, men who have managed to manipulate events to their own benefit, following their own interests to feather their own nests. I must reiterate the dangers of generalisation. There are public men, especially, though not exclusively, in the smaller and poorer Associations and lesser positions, who are genuinely public spirited, but the majority of the really powerful "leaders" are of the type depicted here.

The Influence of the Japanese Occupation

The rapid social changes of the last few years have demonstrated this very clearly. The old type of leadership, based upon independently acquired personal wealth and often imbued with genuine public-spirit, is declining. It is a change of profound significance, but it has gone largely unperceived by outsiders. Probably the greatest single factors, if such manysided forces can be termed single factors, were the Japanese occupation and its aftermath.

The Japanese had long been enemies of China. Since 1937 at least they had been waging a peculiarly aggressive war on Chinese soil. Any sort of friendly gesture towards them was therefore an intolerable offence. Nevertheless quite a large number of those men whom the Sarawak Chinese had been used to regard as pillars of their society turned out to be collaborators. According to tradition a Chinese leader faced by disaster must choose death before dishonour. It was not necessary that all should lay down their lives, but most people at least refused to co-operate or escaped into the jungle. This was not death, though it was danger and it was discomfort. Some of the leading Chinese preferred dishonour to discomfort.[1] The most unfortunate thing of all has been the continued or even increased prosperity and power of these gentlemen since the liberation. I have permission to quote from the unpublished autobiography of the late Mr. J. B. Archer, Chief Secretary of the Government of Sarawak:

> "The real collaborators were men who deliberately joined forces with the enemy and informed on their friends. They were permitted to retain most of their property, they never suffered privation and, in some cases, added to their possessions. Through their tale-bearing, their friends and other loyal persons were tortured, persecuted and killed. I have no sympathy for these collaborators. Owing to the legal difficulties, and for other reasons which would be difficult to explain here, the majority of them were never tried and punished. They are now walking about, free men and, in their own estimation, stainless citizens and pillars of society. Their oleaginous manners and buttery efforts to be well in with the people-who-matter unfortunately deceive the unwary; they are spoken of as such "good chaps", such "decent fellows". The humbler people know better."

---

1. The excuse that they were compelled to collaborate at the point of the bayonet is not acceptable: so many others refused. The other excuse, often put forward, that as Sarawak was a Malay country the Chinese held no responsibility to defend it against aggression is obviously equally unacceptable since the Japanese were aggressors in China long before they attacked Sarawak.

The psychological effects of the misbehaviour of these Chinese "leaders" are profound. Under the present political system the Chinese community undoubtedly needs leaders who can bridge the gap between their community and the Colonial Government, but such leaders must be people who can command respect. Before the occupation the Chinese public regarded their leaders as leaders, despite their faults. Now the long-years established authority of the leadership has collapsed. Although it would be quite unjust to say that all the present holders of social power were collaborators, yet a few of them undoubtedly were, and as long as any of these people still appear on the platforms of public meetings all their colleagues will be tarred with the same brush. At the present time, therefore, the gap between the so-called Chinese "leaders" and the Chinese public which we have already described in structural terms, is made even wider by emotional antagonism. Each side acts in its own way without considering the existence of the other. The "leaders" have only their own cliques to support them, the community is without leadership. For the time being in Sarawak this situation is expressed in no more than a strong undercurrent of feeling, but it is likely to issue in a complete split in the Chinese community. At the same time it produces a double-edged argument between the Chinese and the Colonial Government. From Government's point of view it is a purely Chinese affair, on which government interference would be unwarrantable. But the Chinese public seeing that Government still recognises these men, decide reluctantly that they must be accepted. They dare not say a thing against their "leaders", for fear that the "leaders" will misrepresent them to the Government with which they are apparently in such close contact. The ex-collaborators, on their part, know that their wealth and power is in some ways attached to disgrace. They cannot be community leaders, and must therefore depend upon strengthening their personal followings. Clique building, always, as we have seen, an important part of the process of gaining social power, has therefore become more and more pronounced.

The Significance of the Rural School Boards

The developing conflict between the so-called "leaders" and the Chinese public can also be seen in the rural areas. It is expressed locally in the form of quarrels between the Capitans China and the members of the managing boards of the Chung Hua Schools.[1] In accordance with the situation in Kuching one might expect that the Capitan China would also be Chairman of the local school board. In fact, however, this is usually not so. The deep interest in education which we described above has a chance to show itself in the rural areas where the general public is intensely enthusiastic while the Capitans China, usually the richest men in the districts, are, with a few exceptions, not so keen. The Government's insistence upon annual elections here does give an opportunity for the expression of public opinion. It has become usual to find that after the first year or two the chairmanship of the local school management falls away from the Capitan China.[2] During his term of office each new Chairman strives to compete with his predecessors in activity on behalf of the school, and there thus often develops a kind of rivalry between the new chairman and the Capitan China which eventually accentuates the cleavage between what the Chinese themselves call the "new" and the "old" cliques. The Capitans China, rich and satisfied with the status quo are naturally inclined to be conservative; the Chairmen of the school boards, interested in education, are naturally inclined to be progressive. Before the schools appeared this cleavage was not so conspicuous, but the setting up of the schools has made the educational boards everywhere in the rural districts into platforms from which to challenge the Capitans China.

---

1. In areas where there are no Capitans China the conflict is between the new but local school boards and the old established, unofficial, "leadership" of certain locally powerful individuals.
2. There is no clear way of predicting which people, in structural terms, are likely to become Chairman of School Boards. At present the choice seems to depend entirely upon individual qualities.

For the first time, therefore, there is in the rural districts a possible alternative for the development of leadership, and as the school by its nature is an institution which provides a channel of contact with the Colonial Administration, there exists also the possibility of the development of an alternative line of communication.

The Possibility of Change

With this one, as yet only potential, exception it is difficult to see any way in which ordinary Chinese public opinion in Sarawak can find expression. Elections are held annually as the Administration requires, but the electors know what the final result will be long before they cast their votes. If by some mischance an influential man is not elected, then his name is quietly added to the official lists afterwards, for the system of cliques make certain men indispensable.

At meetings, if the powerful men do not speak, then there is no discussion, for no one dares to make a suggestion before the "leader" opens his mouth. When subscriptions are called for the "leaders" must subscribe first, for no one dares to run the risk of offending them by giving more or giving first.[1]

We have seen how the overseas Chinese community is divided into many smaller groups, each welded together by a number of different types of social relationship. Power in the various groups depends on a similar multiplicity of factors. There is thus no distribution of the different types of social power, and at the same time no check upon any of them. The present Chinese "leaders" are like those small celluloid dolls with leaden feet: even such great events as the Japanese occupation and the subsequent liberation could not turn them down. Within the existing system they are adaptable to any external political situation. It is not surprising, therefore, that they should be staunch opponents of any fundamental change in local Chinese organisation.

With the hoped for speeding up of economic development in Sarawak, however, it is the general opinion that the existing social organisation must be changed. Nearly all the big Associations in which the holders of power exercise their influence are ostensibly based upon differences in dialect, but, as we have seen, their actual foundations are secured by economic interest. At the present time a variety of new Associations based upon occupations are being set up. It seems as if the old dialect Associations are losing their raison d'être. That they remain significant at all is largely to be ascribed to the ambition and continued prestige of certain powerful individuals. The younger generation who have been to school and the educated Chinese can all speak Mandarin and are no longer interested in dialect barriers.[2] They desire to build up a single Chinese community, regardless of differences of origin or sectional interests, but the holders of power are naturally anxious to hold on to the old Associations in which they have the controlling positions. This divergence of view is increasingly becoming the central problem for the oversea Chinese in Sarawak. It is undeniable that social reorganisation is an essential preliminary to the task of building a modern Chinese community. But anyone who

---

1. Newcomers to the Chinese community can easily find a guide to the local social stratification by consulting the lists of subscriptions published in the local press (for famine or flood relief funds in China, for example). Names and amounts usually run more or less strictly in order of social importance.

2. Kuo Yu, the National Language of China, is based mainly upon Mandarin. Developed as a lingua franca for all Chinese it is the medium of instruction in all Chung Hua schools.

advocates reorganisation is immediately accused of subversion by the influential gentlemen who are still regarded as "leaders" of the Chinese. In this way the purely social problems are deliberately given a political flavour, and as, at the present time, this part of the world is madly haunted by political issues such accusations are often only too easily believed.

It is to be noted that should effective political relations ever be established between the British Government and the Chinese People's Government in Peking, considerable realignment of avowed political faith would doubtless follow. But it is important to remember that this would not in itself alter the existing power structure in the Sarawak Chinese community.

X

R E L A T I O N S   W I T H   T H E   M O T H E R   C O U N T R Y

The continued close attachment of the overseas Chinese to their native land has often been remarked. Wherever they are and however long they have been there, Chinese remain Chinese. There is nothing very mysterious about this. Most immigrant communities in foreign lands show signs of homesickness, and maintain links with their mother countries. The British in Australia and the New World named hundreds of places after English, Scottish, Welsh and Irish towns and villages; The New Zealanders to-day talk of Great Britain as "home"; the political solidarity of widely scattered emigrant communities with the home land was amply demonstrated in 1914 and 1939. Irish, Italians and Greeks in the United States, to mention only three examples, write to their kinsmen at home, send money to help towards their maintenance, and return to show off their prosperity if they attain it. Migrants in Africa show similar traits. It needs to be realised that the attachment of the overseas Chinese to their homeland is not a unique phenomenon but rather a normal attribute of any emigrant community in respect to the culture of its original homeland. If the "double loyalty" of the Chinese in the Nan Yang to-day is a political problem it is because there are underlying social and economic problems of considerable magnitude.

This, of course, is a truism. But the social problems themselves are not simple. Most of them have formed the subject matter of the preceding chapters of this book. Briefly it may be said that the strong Chinese attachment to China is the result of a complex of motives arising out of the primary binding obligations of kinship and local patriotism together with the fact that every Chinese who emigrates does so with the fixed intention of returning: the lack of recognised official position in the receiving country, together with racial and cultural distinctness and the whole weight of traditional Chinese cultural pride with its insistence upon publicly affirmed social prestige; the lack of economic opportunity and possibility of social advance for the young. It is these, rather than the "jus sanguinis" of China, or undemonstrable "racial traits", or vague "nationalism", which explain the depth of oversea Chinese patriotic sentiment.

The present chapter contains an analytic description of the numerous ways (social, economic, political, emotional) in which this Chinese attachment to the mother country may be seen in practice.

Social

It may be argued that for the last fifteen hundred years at least the fundamental elements in Chinese rural economy have remained unaltered; throughout this period the essential feature of Chinese social structure has been its basis in an agriculture which relied entirely upon man power organised in kinship groups. Emigration may appear to cut individuals off from their kin at home, but as we saw in Chapter II emigration is never[1] intended to be more than a temporary measure, and in any case groups of kinsmen often travel together or, usually, congregate once more on arrival in the Nan Yang. Kinship ties, the absolutely binding nature of which has been the basic moral obligation of Chinese society, are thus not completely broken even in the physical sense.

Morally they remain of pre-eminent significance. The departure of a single individual from his clan village in China is often a matter of collective responsibility. Kinsmen give him presents for the journey and for the new life; his passage money may be paid, even if he can afford it for himself. This is done as a kind of investment. If the emigrant prospers then it is his duty to share his good fortune with his kinsmen. The value of the gifts received must be repaid. Even regular monthly remittances are often shared between a wider group of kin than the emigrant's own simple family. Failure to send gifts at festival times, especially before the Chinese New Year, causes real shame to an emigrant, and justifiable offence to his relatives. The economic significance of these transactions are studied in more detail below. Here it is enough to point out that morally the overseas Chinese and their kinsmen at home are never separated. On all family occasions, weddings, funerals, birthdays, presents and greetings are exchanged between kinsmen abroad and kinsmen at home, and in the same way between kinsmen in different foreign countries.

Obviously not every oversea Chinese can send gifts to his kin. Some are too poor, some have been absent for so many generations that individual relatives in the home village are no longer known. All, however, have a general responsibility towards the home village or home town as a whole. This may be seen in the attitude towards the ancestral halls or village temples in China. On Petanak Road, Kuching, there is a village of Henghua fishermen, many of whom have the surname Ch'eng. On the walls of every single Ch'eng house hangs a photograph of the Ch'eng ancestral hall which was built in China with the aid of the combined contributions of Ch'eng clan members at home and abroad. When it was finished a photograph was sent to every overseas member. Visitors are told with evident pride: "You see? This is our ancestral hall. We built it."

Overseas Chinese are also asked to join in the annual worship in the ancestral hall which takes place at home. According to custom the organisation of this worship usually falls to each lineage of the clan[2] in turn. In some cases, of course, the members of one of the lineages may have been abroad for several generations, yet the overseas lineage is still bound in duty to provide some service for the worship: perhaps to repair or redecorate the hall, or to provide clothing for the ancestral images. For such things overseas members can contribute money, or may be asked to pay their shares afterwards. Divided up equally the expenditure for each individual is very small, and most are willing, even eager, to pay. Anyone who refuses may be threatened by the others, who will retaliate by refusing to attend funerals or weddings in the offender's family. My own observations on kinship confirmed me in the view, which I have already expressed above, that on the whole it is the poor rather than the rich who are most

---

1. There may be exceptions to this generalisation nowadays. Fukien speaking people in the Nan Yang show a tendency towards international permanent settlement, successful colonists sending for their kinsmen to come out to join them rather than themselves returning home. The earlier chapters have made the more prosperous status of the Fukienese in the Nan Yang quite clear. Members of this group undoubtedly have more to gain by staying. This point, however, needs further study.

2. For these terms see Chapter V.

enthusiastic in such matters.[1]

Interest in home news is never-failing. Small trifles from the home town are more eagerly discussed than important local events. Home news circulates with remarkable speed through correspondence, and through newspapers and journals. Chinese publications from China, are numerous and popular, and the Nan Yang Chinese publications which are in constant demand are concerned mainly with home news. At the present time Singapore is the main centre for Nan Yang Chinese publications, of which the following are available in Sarawak:-

T A B L E   22

CHINESE PUBLICATIONS DEALING WITH HOME NEWS AVAILABLE IN SARAWAK

Dialect Group	Publication	Place Published
Foochow (Henghua included)	Foochow Voice (monthly) Oversea Foochow Journal (twice monthly)	Singapore "
Fukien	Fukien Times, Oversea Edition (monthly)	"
Teochow (Hakka included)	South Seas (twice monthly) Teochow Home News (twice monthly)	" "
Chao An	Chao An Impartial News (daily) Chao An People's News (daily)	Chao An[3] " " [3]
Hainan	The Journal of the Kiung Chow Hwee Kuan Union (The General Hainan Association in British Colonies (monthly)	Singapore

All these newspapers and magazines deal vividly and in detail with the home news of each district. They publish life histories of the famous figures of each dialect group, accounts of the activities of members of the same group in other foreign countries, historical and legendary stories from the home towns, descriptions of the scenery at home with large scale maps and so forth.

1. In recent years overseas Chinese have been approached by clansmen at home who were groaning under harsh Kuomintang taxation, levied not on persons or property but divided according to locality. I know of no overseas Chinese payments for this purpose, however.

2. Published in Chao An, distributed regularly by a Chao An agent in Kuching.

Notices of the transference of property in the home districts, and Chinese local government announcements also appear in these papers. At the same time individual readers can find items of individual interest too, for in the oversea communities the most popular way of extending one's congratulations or sympathy on such occasions as weddings or funerals is to insert a short paragraph in the newspaper. This is not the usual custom in China itself, but nowadays if there is a social function involving both home folk and overseas Chinese then the same method is adopted at home as well. There is no doubt that this new custom serves to strengthen as well as to express social relationships. If one's mother dies in China, one can receive public messages of consolation from one's kinsmen in Malaya, Singapore, Siam, Sarawak, Borneo - everywhere where the papers are read. Friends who had been ignorant learn of the bereavement in this way, and publish their sympathy too, in the next issue. A whole series of such public messages may appear one after the other - sometimes for months on end - until all one's kinsmen and friends, scattered though they may be, have fulfilled their social responsibilities. There is no doubt at all that this continued cementing of personal relationships acts also as a continued strengthening of patriotic sentiment.[1]

Economic

It is the economic aspect of these ties of kinship and local patriotism which probably strikes the outside observer most forcibly. Figures relating to China's balance of trade and the size of remittances from overseas can only give a crude indication of the general situation. The Chinese home currencies have been subject to repeated devaluation over a long period, and comparisons between one year and another have little meaning in terms of real wages or commodity values. Ever since 1877 China has had an unfavourable balance of trade. For many years, however, the remittances sent by the overseas Chinese have helped to bridge the gap. The emigrants, indeed, are equivalent to overseas capital investment. Unfortunately for scientific purposes, it is very difficult to estimate the total amount of these remittances exactly. Sums for family maintenance, subscriptions to famine or flood relief, travelling expenses, gifts, investments, are remitted in a variety of ways, and only those which pass through the banks can be fully accounted for, but even estimates based upon bank returns vary considerably. A recent writer states: "The total of annual oversea remittances during the 'thirties' was variously estimated at U.S. $90 millions to U.S. $150 millions."[2]

The same writer makes the point that it is impossible to deal separately with the different types of remittance from Chinese emigrants. Welfare and war contributions, savings for investment and other business purposes, remittances for support of relatives, have all to be lumped together. The China Handbook[3] 1937-1945 attempts to deal separately with war contributions: "By the end of 1944, a total of C.N. $738,341,331 had been received directly by the Ministry of Finance from the oversea Chinese as their contribution towards the war", but adds rather vaguely: "Besides, the oversea Chinese contributed heavily in the purchasing of Chinese bonds, war planes, trucks, medical supplies and other

---

1. In their presentation of news and their leading articles these overseas publications can adopt a rather more independent line than has been possible for newspapers in China. At the same time they naturally express the interests of the overseas Chinese, and so have rather a special attitude towards affairs at home. Even government officials in the home towns have been known to pay attention to this kind of public opinion abroad, which has thus occasionally been able to check some of the more glaring examples of Kuomintang corruption.

2. Frank M. Temagna: Banking and Finance in China. (Institute of Pacific Relations. New York,) 1942.

   The whole subject of overseas Chinese remittances is a complex one which falls, strictly, outside the scope of this study.

3. China Handbook. (Chinese Ministry of Information. New York) 1947. pp.33.

materials." The Yearbook published by the International Monetary Fund[1] states that personal remittances consisting primarily of remittances for the maintenance of families at home constitute "a comparatively large source of income", but when it comes to exact figures for China has to admit virtual ignorance: "the estimates for personal remittances in 1946 and 1947 are based on data on the numbers of Chinese overseas. It is believed that remittances in 1946 were somewhat higher than in 1947 . . . ", and: "The data for China are based on the number of Chinese nationals living abroad and an estimated yearly average remittance", but this includes "missionary, educational and other benevolent" remittances by private institutions and persons.[2]

For myself I admit freely that I cannot say exactly what sums are remitted, or how they are distributed. It is my opinion that, generally speaking, Chinese tend to exaggerate and Europeans to underestimate their value. All I can do here is to give the official figures of family remittances from Sarawak.

In this colony, as in Malaya and Singapore, family remittances are limited by regulation. No individual may send more than $45 a month. Control is kept by the issue of certificates, and these give a useful method of checking, approximately, the amount of money sent. Between December 1947 and August 1949 395 such certificates were issued in Kuching. The total amount of money sent back to China, in the three years since the Japanese war is estimated as follows :-

T A B L E   23

FAMILY REMITTANCES TO CHINA THROUGH APPROVED COLLECTING AGENTS
(Unit - Straits dollar) 3

Year	Amount
1946 (from July 5th)	$ 85,757.98
1947	134,907.14
1948	77,596.30

These figures, and the number of certificates issued, may appear surprisingly low. It is probably true that not all the money actually sent is accounted for here. On the other hand, even a rough investigation shows that those who actually send money to China are only a small percentage of the total Chinese community. The rural people and most of the labourers are too poor; the rich towkays feel the political situation in China too risky. Remittances come mainly from the middle economic class: the shop-assistants[4] and some of the professional people. The fact that remittances come mostly from the middle economic strata was also noted before the war in the investigation made by

---

1. International Monetary Fund, Balance of Payments Yearbook, (Washington) 1947. p.119.
   An interesting point from this report is the proof that other countries, notably Greece and Italy, also receive a comparatively large part of their income from the personal remittances of emigrants. In 1946 and 1947 U.S. $28 millions and U.S. $21 millions respectively are said to have been remitted in this way to Greece, and U.S. $45 millions and U.S. $34.1 millions to Italy. These are both countries from which emigration owing to economic pressure has taken place on a large scale. There is here a significant indication that the position of the overseas Chinese is not unique, but the natural outcome of emigrant conditions.

2. op.cit. p.35.

3. Figures obtained from the Treasury Dept., Kuching.

4. A group of shop-assistants working together may all want to send family remittances. In such cases their employer, the shop-keeper, often makes an arrangement with a remittance shop for them - himself paying over part of their salaries direct to the remittance shop each month. See below.

Professor T. Chen in 1934. Among one hundred remittance receiving families in China the amount of money received per month was distributed as follows[1]:-

Money Received per Month (in Chinese dollars)	Number of Families
Below $20	17
$20 - $49	49
$50 - $124	21
$125 - $250	13

Thus even before the war a remittance receiving family in China obtained on an average about $53 only each month (i.e. about £4).

The economic relationship between Chinese at home and overseas is maintained far less through the banks than through the remittance shops. Their position as the social machinery through which the complicated system of remittance mainly works can best be understood from a consideration of their origin and development. The Chinese who first came overseas belonged mostly to the labouring class. Driven by want, their one aim was to secure enough money to keep their families at home from starvation. The ideal, if all went well, was that each emigrant should return himself with his fortune in his pocket, settle down and live happily ever after. But this did not often happen. Instead, money might be sent little by little, while the emigrant remained, saving and scraping, far from home. At a time when postal services and banks did not exist, the usual method was for each group of people (a clan or locality group as a rule) to select one honest and reliable man from their number who might be entrusted with carrying their contributions home. From this early beginning there developed the system of "travelling merchants[2]: men whose two-fold occupation was to do ordinary business for themselves on the one hand, and to render services, such as taking back money and correspondence, and bringing out relatives, for their clients in the Nan Yang, on the other. Eventually many of the grocery shops in the rural districts in the Nan Yang became interested in this kind of business. From time to time the local Chinese labourers would send in small sums of money. When a fair amount had accumulated the grocer would send one of his employees or relatives back to China with the money. If it happened that the agent was ready to go before a certain labourer had managed to save enough, the shop would often be prepared to advance a loan, allowing the client to repay it gradually as he could (with a certain amount of interest).

The second stage of the development of the remittance business saw the emergence of special remittance shops, which have now almost entirely replaced the older system. At the present time there are large numbers of these shops, with widely scattered but closely related branch agencies throughout the Nan Yang. Remittance shops do not only send money, in the cold impersonal way of banks, but, run by men of the same dialect group (and usually the same locality or even clan) as the senders they provide other, more intimate, services too. Letters can be attached to the remittances, even written for the illiterate, news from home can be obtained, personal worries caused by distance and loneliness can be alleviated, advice and material help are often forthcoming. This personal, intimate, relationship between the remittance shops and their clients explains their continued success in the face of the more efficient, but colder, services of banks and post offices.[3]

1. Ta Chen: Emigrant Communities in South China. (New York) 1939. p.83.
2. Cp. p. 38 Note 1 above.
3. Where a Chinese bank, run by members of a particular dialect group, has set up branches in the Nan Yang, however, it seems to attract more clients from that dialect group than do the remittance shops. At the present time remittance shops flourish mainly in the Fukien, Teochow, Hainan speaking areas. Cantonese and Hakkas are well provided for by various branches of the provincial bank of Kwangtung, and in their areas very few remittance shops are to be found.

The business methods of the remittance shops are difficult for an outsider to comprehend. Their managers all carry on other lines of business at the same time, and it is this fact which perhaps explains their present prosperity. The instability of the exchange rates since the liberation may also have something to do with their continued success in the face of intense mutual competition.

In Kuching there are 44 shops which have been registered as approved agents for the collection of family remittances for China. Among them only two or three are really popular. The rest are rather small scale businesses; some, indeed, have actually closed down.[1]

Political

I have suggested that the continued strength of kinship ties is a factor in the maintenance of sentiments of Chinese patriotism. The destination of some of the remittances, too, shows this patriotism, for not all go to kinsmen, Often they are contributions to national funds, as for flood or famine relief, or to the coffers of various political parties at home. Chinese patriotism is expressed both in emotional and in practical terms. From the practical point of view it is to be seen in the continuous lively interest and intervention in home politics. It was not for nothing that Dr. Sun Yat-Sen called the overseas Chinese the mothers of the Revolution of 1911.

Partly because their racial conspicuousness and political disfranchisement in the countries of their adoption has induced them to turn to home politics "faute de mieux"; partly because of the "jus sanguinis" determining Chinese nationality; partly because they were in closer contact with the then new ideas of the West; partly because they shared the common exiles' longing for perfection at home; partly because some of them came abroad as political refugees - for all these reasons the overseas Chinese have played what appears at first sight to have been an almost disproportionate part in home politics. In the early stages of the 1911 Revolution all the four leaders of the Tung-Ming-Hui were overseas Chinese. Nearly all the important decisions were made outside China. Nearly all the donations come from abroad. Dr. Sun's own sojourns overseas are well known. From 1911 until to-day the overseas Chinese have been involved in almost every political event in China, represented at almost every political meeting. From the very beginning the overseas Chinese were thought to fall under the programme of the Kuomingtang Government. Branches of the KMT party organisation were set up everywhere in the Nan Yang, and members were recruited in great numbers. This in itself accentuated the already quick sensibility of the overseas Chinese to the vicissitudes of home politics. Almost any political event in China now produced its reactions in the overseas communities. Local politics were relatively ignored, but disputes on matters of home politics often appeared to be even more serious overseas than in China itself.

Sarawak, however, remained a backwater. Geographical isolation and the lack of adequate educational facilities under the Rajahs meant that the Chinese there kept aloof from home politics. The enthusiam for the overthrow of the Manchus in 1911 which swept the other overseas communities resulted in Sarawak only in the setting up of a kind of "reading room" which sold books and pamphlets for propaganda purposes. (That was the result of a visit paid by Mr Wang Ching-Wei, later a famous KMT leader and notorious collaborator during the Sino-Japanese war). After 1930 when the Japanese began to invade Manchuria and the movement to raise funds to help the mother country was at white heat in the Nan Yang, the Chinese in Sarawak did play some part, sending con-

---

1. According to figures given by the Nan Yang Chinese Exchange and Remittance Association,* the total number of remittance shops in the Federation of Malaya is about 1,500. In Singapore there are 146 remittance shops, distributed among the dialect groups as follows: Fukien 61, Teochow 45, Hainan 33, Cantonese and Hakka (combined shops) 7. The total number of remittance shops in Siam in 1947 was 121: Teochow 76, Hainan 26, Hakka 12, Cantonese, 5, Fukien 2.

* Annual report of Nan Yang Chinese Exchange and Remittance Association,(Singapore) 1947. pp.2,11,95-104.

tributions and despatching delegates to the meeting of the General   Association of Overseas Chinese in Singapore.

Since the liberation things have changed. At the request of the overseas Chinese Chinese community the Chinese Government opened its first Consulate in Kuching in the spring of 1948. Before that Sarawak received two visits, one from the Consul-General from Singapore, and the other from a special commission from the headquarters of the Kuomintang in Nanking. Since this was the first visit they had ever received from any Chinese government officials, the overseas community made every effort to pay him the highest respect, and a large sum of money was collected and spent in entertainment. Private information suggests, though it may exaggerate, that on the Consul-General alone the Chinese public spent almost $50,000. Yet, during their visits, all that these two important gentlemen could give in return was a little half-hearted hand-shaking, and some empty words and promises. One significant result was a-chieved, however, in the recruitment of members for the KMT and the setting up of a branch organisation in Kuching, called the Chinese Oversea Club.

We have already seen how almost every prosperous Chinese in the Nan Yang desires to attach to himself some odour of officialdom. The Kuomintang was not slow to take advantage of this weakness. It has thus become generally understood that one joins a political party not for reasons of political convic-tion but solely in order to gain "face". For example, when the special commissioner mentioned above came to Sarawak his task was not to convince the lo-cal Chinese that Kuomintang policy was right, or just, or even advantageous; he simply had to give people "face". He presented each of the Chinese leaders with a photograph, or a letter, or some calligraphy of one or other of the Kuomintang leaders; on each gift the recipient found his name inscribed, and himself addressed in the traditional Chinese way as "elder brother". This was very flattering. There were large number of Kuomintang leaders, and each one of them anxious to build up as big a clique as possible, so there were plenty of photographs and letters to go round and the wealthy Chinese of Kuching turn-ed into something like "autograph collectors". In other words it was largely in order to show off his official connection by a lavish display of photo-graphs and mementos to the Chinese world of Sarawak that some of these pros-perous Chinese joined the Kuomintang. In addition, of course, there were those who were moved by a desire to publicize their loyalty to China. These were mainly people whose relations with the Japanese during the occupation had been, to say the least, questionable. The net result was that in 1947 the Kuomin-tang secured a new overseas base and about sixty new members in Sarawak.

A further result has been the confounding of politics with personal feuds and public dishonesty. This is not difficult to understand: in China the only party which has succeeded in standing out against the Kuomintang has been the Communist party. Thus the epithet "Communist" is hurled against anyone who dares to oppose the Kuomintang members in Kuching. Consequently it was the coming of the Kuomintang which created the so-called "communist element" in Sarawak.

It is frequently suggested that the men through whom all the political activities of overseas Chinese communities are engineered are the Chinese Con-suls. This is certainly not entirely true of Sarawak. On the contrary, the consul is largely dependent upon the locally influential Chinese. Although consular salaries and allowances are quite adequate, in actual fact they are not fully drawn upon. The local Chinese community provides almost everything their Consul and his staff need: from a mattress for his bed to the expenses of his cocktail parties, not to mention his residence and his motor car. For all these things the consul relies upon these Chinese leaders who raise the money, and his authority and prestige are therefore largely at their disposal Not long ago the first consul left Sarawak for America. Thereupon a certain leading Chinese in Kuching sent a telegram to the Minister for Foreign Affairs in China, recommending the promotion to the position of secretary of one of the consulate employees over whom he himself had full control. The Minister, I have been told, began to wonder who was really the Consul he appointed. He wondered still more, when he realised that this telegram had been sent in the then most confidential government code.

Emotional

The emotional appeal of China means different things to different people, according to their ages, situations and standards of education. But, despite this variety of meaning, the idea of the existence of a mother country, vague though it may be to some, at least gives every oversea Chinese a sense of security, the feeling that there is always, somewhere, some day, a place to which he belongs, to which he can go.

For the traditionally minded, China is the place to die. In old age they think only of returning home. Some insist that only in China can one have a proper funeral; others declare that it is morally right to die in the place of one's birth. Whatever reason is actually expressed the sentiments spring from the strength of an agriculturally based culture, with its deep attachment to the soil. Unfortunately there is no such opportunity for everybody to go back to China to touch the soil of the mother country before he closes his eyes. Most of the exiles die in their foreign land, unknown to their relatives at home. This, the most dreadful calamity, is a continual topic of conversation among the elderly rural people in Sarawak. It is often said that of every ten who go abroad, only one returns. This is bitter reality, and it must be faced.

To the local born China is a sphinx. It is often suggested that the local born are likely to be less moved by Chinese nationalism than the recent immigrants, for they have received a more western type of education and their personal roots are not in China. But in fact this does not necessarily follow. Local born and China born, they are both Chinese; the only difference lies in the flexibility of sentiment. In certain respects the nationalism of the local born is even stronger than that of the Chinese educated. This is not difficult to understand: to the China born Chinese, the new foreign country is still mysterious and inviting; they have been peeping at it, but they still cannot grasp its reality. But the foreign land is no mystery to a local born Chinese - he speaks the foreign language, he has met a great number of foreign people - what he wants to explore now is the mystery of China. His idea of China is probably quite different from that of his China born friends. He may reject their boastful descriptions, or he may project his own wishes upon his motherland and imagine her as something far more desirable than she really is. Either way, he feels he must see for himself.

The mystery of the sphinx causes mixed feelings in the minds of the local born. On the one hand they take pride in the idea of their mother country, on the other hand they wonder why she should not be modern and strong. Many have tried hard to read books about China, and have carefully followed the events of her contemporary history; a few have even set out to learn to read and write the small insect-like Chinese characters which they have ignored since their childhood. Disheartened at their slow progress they may give up, saying to themselves that it is better not to be closely interested in China, but whenever they feel frustrated in other matters the motherland appeals once more as a kind of emotional compensation. No matter what happens to the individual abroad, so long as there is "China" everything will be all right. Here, too, is a source not only of individual satisfaction, but of social unity. Over and over again arguments between Chinese abroad are settled when one points to his face or his hand and says: "After all, the colour is the same. Why should we quarrel?" It is the yellow colour which implies the China with which they are all associated.[1]

For the younger generation their future ambitions are what matters. If the local situation can offer them suitable openings for really satisfying occupations then they are likely to settle down. Mere business opportunity is not enough; what they need is a chance to be of service, and to play a meaningful part in community life. In Sarawak at present, however, there seem to be but five possibilities for the young: the English educated, with matriculation, can become a government clerk: the Chinese educated can become a teacher in a Chinese school; the wealthy can go into business; those who though neither wealthy nor educated are yet physically strong can grow and tap rubber; those who are none of these things can become shop assistants. In the

---

1. This habit of referring to colour may also be developed as a reaction to the notorious colour consciousness of most Europeans in the Colonies.

last resort all depend upon rubber. It is not surprising that so many young people are unemployed. And it is not surprising that in their frustration they turn to China. There at least there is a greater variety of opportunity, and there to-day they see at last the chance of unprecedented and unlimited community development.

A major purpose of this study has been to show that the present situation of the Chinese in Sarawak is the outcome of economic and social conditions which can be scientifically observed, analysed and understood. There is nothing mysterious, nothing incomprehensible about them. The same is true of Chinese ties with the homeland. Official preoccupation with "double loyalty" sometimes seems to suggest that the attachment which the overseas Chinese show to China is something peculiarly inexplicable. It is argued that it is impossible fully to rely upon immigrants who manifest so strong an attachment to their homeland. Not until their sentiments change will they deserve to be trusted. But if these sentiments are nurtured by the existing circumstances of the colonial environment they cannot be expected to change until the environment itself is different. In other words, it is useless to wait for attitudes to alter first. Only by giving the immigrants a change to develop a stake in the country, by enabling them to take a genuine part in local affairs and share fully in local responsibilities can one begin to create a new set of circumstances which will make it possible for the immigrant community to develop a new set of sentiments towards the land of their adoption.

A P P E N D I C E S

Editorial Note.

Dr. T'ien's original manuscript contains three Appendices only one   of
which is published here.

APPENDIX 1.   The Early History of the Chinese in Sarawak.

This is an account based on documentary sources of very uneven
quality. Its value, as the author himself emphasises is chiefly bib-
liographical. A copy of the manuscript will be retained by the Department of Anthropology, London School of Economics, and will be
available on application to the Head of the Department.

APPENDIX 2.   The Hakka Kongsi in Borneo.

This is an account, based mainly on Dutch and Chinese sources, of
the history and organisation of the Chinese gold mining community in
West Borneo. As in the case of Appendix 1 a copy of the manuscript
will be retained by the Department of Anthropology, London School of
Economics, but it is also hoped to obtain independent publication
elsewhere.

APPENDIX 3.   The Chinese Population of Sarawak : Dialect Groups

(See overleaf pp. 90-91)

	Total of All Groups			CANTONESE		FOOCHOW		HAKKA (includes Kheh)	
	PRS.	MALE	FEMALE	MALE	FEMALE	MALE	FEMALE	MALE	FEMALE
CENSUS DISTRICT OF:-									
LUNDU	1903	1102	801	84	60	–	–	536	429
BAU	7222	4099	3123	72	53	5	3	3639	2820
SERIAN	7602	4348	3254	91	52	16	9	3555	2694
KUCHING RURAL	23695	13106	10589	237	174	136	61	9443	7741
KUCHING MUNICIPAL	21699	11819	9880	862	775	383	258	2461	2162
FIRST DIVISION	62121	34474	27647	1346	1104	540	331	19534	15846
CENSUS DISTRICT OF:-									
SIMANGGANG	2939	1768	1171	39	25	7	2	693	408
LUBOK ANTU	1384	796	588	8	2	–	–	614	452
SARIBAS	2047	1240	807	43	18	18	4	546	379
KALAKA	1725	1093	632	88	50	172	44	163	95
SECOND DIVISION	8095	4897	3198	178	95	197	50	2016	1334
CENSUS DISTRICT OF:-									
LOWER RAJANG	18723	10608	8115	1736	1483	7897	5846	136	131
SIBU RURAL	25565	13584	11981	1550	1581	10723	9180	101	111
SIBU MUNICIPAL	6201	3529	2672	402	284	1806	1262	197	172
KANOWIT	3652	2006	1646	916	809	574	408	49	30
KAPIT	1392	847	545	56	29	361	217	60	39
OYA – DALAT	1349	833	516	83	32	151	70	43	28
MUKAH	2017	1225	792	97	47	264	108	56	48
THIRD DIVISION	58899	32632	26267	4840	4265	21776	17091	642	559
CENSUS DISTRICT OF:-									
BINTULU	2056	1213	843	121	108	482	323	63	47
MIRI RURAL	2586	1525	1061	174	129	9	3	891	628
MIRI MUNICIPAL	6879	4008	2871	1149	891	33	14	1696	1260
BARAM	2682	1577	1105	41	21	612	475	271 ·	160
FOURTH DIVISION	14203	8323	5880	1485	1149	1136	815	2921	2095
CENSUS DISTRICT OF:-									
LIMBANG	900	524	376	59	41	5	4	98	64
LAWAS	940	542	398	36	24	1	–	112	88
FIFTH DIVISION	1840	1066	774	95	65	6	4	210	152
SARAWAK	145158	81392	63766	7944	6678	23655	18291	25423	19986

THE CHINESE POPULATION OF SARAWAK: DIALECT GROUPS.

(From the Census Report, 1947).

HENGHUA (includes Hokchia)		HOKKIEN (includes Fukien and Chao An)		HAILAM (Hainan)		KWANGSI		LUICHOW		TEOCHOW (CH'AOCHOW)		OTHER OR UNSPECIFIED CHINESE	
MALE	FEMALE	MALE	FEMALE	MALE	FEMALE	MALE	FEMALE	MALE	FEMALE	MALE	FEMALE	MALE	FEMALE
–	–	39	25	52	34	–	–	147	94	244	159	–	–
17	11	59	49	111	67	4	–	21	7	159	114	12	9
5	3	271	217	104	57	16	6	13	12	252	178	25	26
75	15	1164	1133	221	120	10	4	263	129	1529	1198	28	14
1103	891	3194	3113	891	588	19	12	81	37	2675	1980	150	64
1200	920	4727	4537	1379	866	49	22	525	279	4859	3627	215	113
–	–	186	130	84	51	3	–	6	4	750	551	–	–
–	–	7	4	5	4	–	–	–	–	162	126	–	–
1	–	130	70	52	39	–	–	10	3	439	294	1	–
–	–	406	323	115	46	8	3	33	18	76	36	32	17
1	–	729	527	256	140	11	3	49	25	1427	1007	33	17
24	12	677	552	41	16	2	5	3	2	82	57	10	11
973	905	200	179	14	10	–	1	1	–	21	12	1	2
92	55	743	714	100	62	31	18	7	1	148	99	3	5
30	27	377	354	16	5	5	–	19	4	16	9	4	–
1	–	349	257	5	2	–	–	1	–	9	1	5	–
26	12	443	324	59	30	–	–	2	2	26	18	–	–
4	4	578	438	24	10	–	–	10	2	190	135	2	–
1150	1015	3367	2818	259	135	38	24	43	11	492	331	25	18
1	–	151	117	38	22	3	2	7	4	329	206	18	14
1	–	282	188	49	36	2	1	3	–	94	67	20	9
44	15	602	395	294	176	6	–	6	3	119	82	59	35
5	4	491	336	64	43	–	–	7	4	86	61	–	1
51	19	1526	1036	445	277	11	3	23	11	628	416	97	59
–	–	275	209	44	28	2	–	–	–	26	20	15	10
–	–	304	234	26	16	13	4	8	3	36	21	6	8
–	–	579	443	70	44	15	4	8	3	62	41	21	18
2402	1954	10928	9361	2409	1462	124	56	648	329	7468	5424	391	225

London School of Economics Monographs on Social Anthropology series

Series Editor: Charles Stafford

With over 70 volumes published since 1949, including classic work by Gell, Barth, Leach and Firth, the LSE Monographs now form one of the most prestigious series in the discipline of Anthropology. Presenting scholarly work from all branches of Social Anthropology the series continues to build on its history with both theoretical and ethnographic studies of the contemporary world.

74. Between China and Europe
Person, Culture and Emotion in Macao
João de Pina-Cabral

73. The Earth Shakers of Madagascar
An Anthropological Study of Authority, Fertility and Creation
Oliver Woolley

72. Chinese Sociologics
An Anthropological Account of Alienation and Social Reproduction
P. Steven Sangren

71. The Performance of Gender
An Anthropology of Everyday Life in a South Indian Fishing Village
Cecilia Busby

70. Arguments with Ethnography
Comparative Approaches to History, Politics and Religion
Ioan M. Lewis

69. Those Who Play with Fire
Gender, Fertility and Transformation in East and Southern Africa
Henrietta L. Moore, Todd Sanders and Bwire Kaare

68. Conceiving Persons
Ethnographies of Procreation, Fertility and Growth
Edited by Peter Z. Loizos and P. Heady

67. The Art of Anthropology
Essays and Diagrams
Alfred Gell (Edited by Eric Hirsch)

66. Leadership and Change in the Western Pacific
Edited by Richard Feinberg and Karen Ann Watson-Gegeo

65. Hierarchy and Egalitarianism
Castle, Class and Power in Sinhalese Peasant Society
Tamara Gunasekera

64. The Harambee Movement in Kenya
Self-help, Development and Education among the Kamba of Kitui District
Martin J. D. Hill

63. Society and Politics in India
Essays in a Comparative Perspective
Andre Beteille

62. The Power of Love
The Moral Use of Knowledge amongst the Amuesha of Central Peru
Fernando Santos-Granero

61. Making Sense of Hierarchy
Cognition as Social Process in Fiji
Christina Toren

60. The Social Practice of Symbolization
An Anthropological Analysis
Ivo Strecker

59. Gods on Earth
The Management of Religious Experience and Identity in a North Indian Pilgrimage Centre
Peter van der Veer

58. Ritual, History and Power
Selected Papers in Anthropology
Maurice Bloch

57. Sacrifice and Sharing in the Philippine Highlands
Religion and Society among the Buid of Mindoro
Thomas P. Gibson

56. Communication, Social Structure and Development in Rural Malaysia
A Study of Kampung Kuala Bera
William D. Wilder

55. Forest Traders
A Socio-Economic Study of the Hill Pandaram
Brian Morris

54. Ma' Betisék Concepts of Living Things
Wazir-Jahan Karim

53. White Nile Arabs
Political Leadership and Economic Change
Abbas Ahmed Mohamed

52. Knowledge of Illness in Sepik Society
A Study of the Gnau, New Guinea
Gilbert Lewis

51. Metamorphosis of the Cassowaries
Umeda Society, Language and Ritual
Alfred Gell

50. Choice and Change
Edited by John Davis

49. Beyond the Village
Local Politics in Madang, Papua New Guinea
Louise Morauta

48. Land and Family in Pisticci
J. Davis

47. West Indian Migration
The Montserrat Case
Stuart B. Philpott

46. Uncertainties in Peasant Farming
A Colombian Case
Sutti Ortiz

45. Pioneers in the Tropics
The Political Organization of Japanese in an Immigrant Community in Brazil
Philip Staniford

44. Political Systems of Highland Burma
A Study of Kachin Social Structure
E. R. Leach

43. **Tribal Innovators**
Tswana Chiefs and Social Change 1795–1940
Isaac Schapera

42. **The Political Structure of the Chinese Community in Cambodia**
W. E. Willmott

41. **Report on the Iban**
Derek Freeman

40. **Time and Social Structure and Other Essays**
Meyer Fortes

39. **Take Out Hunger**
Two Case Studies of Rural Development in Basutoland
Sandra Wallman

38. **Anthropology and Social Change**
Lucy Mair

37. **Kinship and Marriage among the Anlo Ewe**
G. K. Nukunya

36. **Christianity and the Shona**
Marshall Murphree

35. **The Keresan Bridge**
A Problem in Pueblo Ethnology
Robin Fox

34. **Kinship and Social Organization**
W. H. R. Rivers

33. **Chinese Lineage and Society**
Fukien and Kwantung
Maurice Freedman

32. **Kinship and Economic Organization in Rural Japan**
Chie Nakane

31. **The Muslim Matrimonial Court in Singapore**
Judith Djamour

30. **Saints and Fireworks**
Religion and Politics in Rural Malta
Jeremy Boissevain

29. **Malay Peasant Society in Jelebu**
M. G. Swift

28. **Essays on Social Organization and Values**
Raymond Firth

27. **A New Maori Migration**
Rural and Urban Relations in Northern New Zealand
Joan Metge

26. **Kinship and Marriage in a New Guinea Village**
H. Ian Hoghin

25. **Conflict and Solidarity in a Guianese Plantation**
Chandra Jayawardena

24. **Legal Institutions in Manchu China**
A Sociological Analysis
Sybille van der Sprenkel

23. **Marsh Dwellers of the Euphrates Delta**
S. M. Salim

22. **Rethinking Anthropology**
E. R. Leach

21. **Malay Kinship and Marriage in Singapore**
Judith Djamour

20. **Social Status and Power in Java**
L. H. Palmier

19. **Political Leadership among Swat Pathans**
Fredrik Barth

18. **Lineage Organization in South-Eastern China**
Maurice Freedman

17. **Indigenous Political Systems of Western Malaya**
J. M. Gullick

16. **Studies in Applied Anthropology**
Lucy Mair
Replaced by Volume No. 38

15. **Two Studies of Kinship in London**
Raymond Firth

14. **Chinese Spirit-Medium Cults in Singapore**
Alan J. A. Elliott

13. **Changing Lapps**
Gutorm Gjessing

12. **The Chinese of Sarawak**
A Study of Social Structure
Ju-K'ang Tien

11. **The Ethnic Composition of Tswana Tribes**
Isaac Schapera

10. **Akokoaso**
A Survey of a Gold Coast Village
W. H. Beckett

9. **Tribal Legislation among the Tswana of the Bechuanaland Protectorate**
Isaac Schapera
Replaced by Volume No. 43

8. **A Demographic Study of an Egyptian Province (Sharqiya)**
A. M. Ammar

7. **Housekeeping among Malay Peasants**
Rosemary Firth

6. **Land Tenure of an Ibo Village in South-Eastern Nigeria**
M. M. Green

5. **Marriage and the Family among the Yakö in South-Eastern Nigeria**
Darryl Forde

4. **The Political System of the Anuak of the Anglo-Egyptian Sudan**
E. E. Evans-Pritchard

3. **Social and Economic Organization of the Rowanduz Kurds**
Edmund Leach

1 & 2. **The Work of the Gods in Tikopia**
Raymond Firth

Printed in the United Kingdom
by Lightning Source UK Ltd.
134466UK00001B/1-2/A